Reconciling Journey

Reconciling Journey

A Devotional Workbook for Lesbian and Gay Christians

MICHAL ANNE PEPPER

THE PILGRIM PRESS  CLEVELAND

THIS WORK IS DEDICATED TO THE MEMORY OF MY PARENTS, LaVada AND Ken Pepper, WHO INTRODUCED ME TO CHRIST AND WHO ENCOURAGED ME TO BE AUTHENTIC.

The Pilgrim Press, 700 Prospect Avenue, Cleveland, Ohio 44115-1100
pilgrimpress.com
© 2003 by Michal Anne Pepper

Unless otherwise noted, biblical quotations are from the New Revised Standard Version of the Bible,
© 1989 by the Division of Christian Education of the National Council of the Churches of Christ
in the U.S.A. and are used by permission. Adaptations have been made for inclusivity.

Printed in the United States of America on acid-free paper

08   07   06   05   04   03   5   4   3   2   1

Library of Congress Cataloging-in-Publication Data
Pepper, Michal Anne, 1952–
    Reconciling journey : a devotional workbook for lesbian and gay Christians / Michal Anne Pepper.
      p. cm.
    ISBN 0-8298-1569-4 (pbk.)
    1. Christian gays—Prayer-books and devotions—English.   I. Title.
BV4596.G38P46   2003
261.8'35766—dc22
                                              2003060866

Contents

Gathering and Invocation   vii

WEEK ONE   My Faith Story   1

WEEK TWO   Images of God   13

WEEK THREE   Reconciled in Jesus Christ   23

WEEK FOUR   The Inspired and Inspiring Word   35

WEEK FIVE   Making Ourselves Available to God   51

WEEK SIX   We Learn to Hear God   63

WEEK SEVEN   Members of the Body of Christ   77

WEEK EIGHT   Our Witness to Living in Christ   89

WEEK NINE   Witness Inspired by the Holy Spirit   103

Benediction and Dispersal   117

Resources (Annotated)   121

GATHERING AND INVOCATION

Several years ago, I received a call from the vice president of Honesty-Dallas, the organization of gay, lesbian, and bisexual Southern Baptists. She asked me to develop a program to help their members reconcile their sexual orientation with their Christian faith. At the time, I had a counseling psychology practice in Dallas and had worked with many lesbian and gay persons struggling to come to terms with their sexual orientation. My clinical experience was that people could not overcome religiously inspired internalized homophobia with therapy alone.

I didn't think I was qualified to create such a program, but I agreed to do it because the need was so great. I developed a ten-week program. Over the next few years, I led two or three of these groups a year. This workbook was born from that experience. I am indebted to the women and men who talked and prayed with me in those groups for the growth of this workbook. Their lives and their faith gave it its shape and spirit.

The most basic assumption of this workbook is that Christian discipleship is the foundation of our lives. Our sexual orientation is an important part of who we are. Our intimate relationships are significant components of our lives. However, these exercises assume that our relationship with God defines who we are: beloved children of God in Christ.

Sometimes as we struggle to be authentic persons in a culture that is hostile to us and to those we love, the oppression and abuse we endure every day seems to define our lives. The systemic evil of discrimination appears to be the primary force shaping our lives. But God is more powerful than any discrimination, and God is more powerful than any human institution. Christ lives in us and we live in him. Christ shapes us in his image even though we live in an oppressive world.

The second assumption underlying this workbook is that the good news of Jesus Christ is powerful enough to free us from the life-destroying urges we imbibe from the rampant homophobia in our churches and in our culture. Consequently, I have structured the workbook to help us know that good news.

Because the radical right so continuously attacks us, our immediate and natural response is to defend ourselves. But when we spend our time and energy defending ourselves, our lives are shaped by the agenda of those who condemn us, not by Jesus Christ. Therefore, this workbook spends very little time providing a lesbian and gay Christian defense against those who attack us. Instead, the focus of this workbook is the good news that the Son of God loved us and gave himself for us.

When I initially agreed to develop a program for Honesty, I had no idea how God would use that task to redirect my life. My role as group leader led me into more pastoral care than psychological care. Over time, I became aware that God was calling me into a different form of ministry. I eventually entered seminary, was ordained as a minister of the Christian Church (Disciples of Christ), and am currently pastor of University Christian

Church of Berkeley in Berkeley, California. My transition from psychologist to pastor has deepened my understanding of Christian discipleship and the underlying theological issues. My hope and prayer is that this workbook benefits from that deepened understanding.

PEOPLE WHO COULD FIND THIS WORKBOOK HELPFUL

Eventually, many lesbian and gay Christians come to a crossroads: we can either embrace our sexual orientation, or we can embrace our Christian discipleship. To do both seems impossible. Some of us acknowledge our sexual orientation and grow into mature gay and lesbian persons. We learn to date and find a partner. We develop a community of like-minded people. We learn to be comfortable with who we are and whom we love. However, that comfort comes at a cost—the cost of our Christian faith. In order to shield ourselves from the church's intense homophobia, we separate ourselves from Christianity. We quit going to church. We put our Bibles on the shelf. We quit praying. We abandon any spiritual disciplines we once practiced.

We have been deeply hurt by the church. As one friend of mine says, "Christianity is toxic for gay and lesbian people," So we put "all that stuff" behind us. But in leaving Christianity behind, we are left with a big hole—the big God-shaped hole our faith once filled. Some of us fill that hole with drugs, alcohol, or lots of sex. For others of us, we try to fill that hole with projects like home improvement, bodybuilding, or creating the perfect wardrobe. Many of us look to partners or friends to fill that hole. Still others of us throw ourselves into our careers.

Abandoned spiritual disciplines create another void. We may have been accustomed to praying about important decisions in our lives. We looked for God's guidance and were confident that our welfare was important to God. But losing Christianity meant we lost this resource of prayer as well. We no longer seek God's guidance about jobs or family or dating. We no longer go to God for comfort, refreshment, hope, or peace. We have to find those things elsewhere.

Some of us stay faithful as disciples of Christ, but neglect that most important part of ourselves: our capacity to love another human being and to create a life together. We are convinced of God's claim on our lives as Christians. That claim may even be some form of ordained or lay ministry. We are not willing to turn our backs on God or the church. Our hearts are completely captured by our work in the church. We cannot imagine doing anything to jeopardize our life in Christ, our life in the church.

So we deny our sexual orientation. Sometimes we even deny our sexual orientation to ourselves. We live deep in the closet. We may marry someone of the opposite sex and have children. Or we stay celibate and away from other lesbian and gay people. Our only acknowledgement of who we are may be furtive trips to gay bars when we are out of town. Those of us who choose this path may tell ourselves that we are making a sacrifice. We tell ourselves that our isolation is the cost God extracts from us as faithful servants. We want to be willing servants, and so we sacrifice our lives as whole people to God's service.

Some of us, straight and gay, *are* called to celibacy. A few Christians are asked to sacrifice sexual relationships to God's larger purpose for us. And that sacrifice is initially painful. But it doesn't stay painful. When we make a sacrifice that God calls us to make, we are carried through the pain into joy. Our loneliness is transformed into peace. When we give God something God wants, our initial pain resolves into divine delight.

But when we give God something others want us to give, our initial pain spirals into the dull ache of depression. We wrestle with the pain. We wrestle with our loneliness. And finally, our pain and our loneliness turn into depression and despair. Instead of knowing the joy of serving our Lord with gladness, we drag ourselves from one task to the other. We have made a sacrifice that God does not want from us.

Some of us, rather than choosing either sexual orientation or Christianity, make a choice that puts us somewhere in the middle of these two groups. We acknowledge our sexual orientation. We learn to be comfortable with who we are. But we never quite let go of our faith. We may find some way to stay involved with church. Or we may continue to read the Bible and pray. We come to an uneasy truce within ourselves. We say we know God made us and loves us as lesbian and gay persons. We say we are comfortable with who we are. But underneath that brave assertion lurks a nagging question: *What if they are right? What if homosexuality is a sin?*

Those of us who grew up in conservative churches are particularly afflicted by this question. We were so brainwashed by a particular view of God that no amount of education or reason can overcome the intensity of those early images and stories. So we are haunted by the question: *What if they are right?*

This workbook can be used by people in each of these groups: those who have disavowed Christianity, but would like to come home; those who have disavowed their sexual orientation, but would like to come out; and those who are both out and at home, but are haunted by the question: *What if they are right?* The exercises in this workbook are designed to deepen your Christian discipleship by integrating your sexual orientation and your faith in Jesus Christ.

WHAT IS THIS WORKBOOK?

This workbook has nine weeks of devotional exercises. Each week invites you to revisit some theological issue or spiritual practice. The first week you create a map of your spiritual journey. The second week you explore your images of God. The third week you revisit sin, confession and forgiveness, and the reconciliation of Jesus Christ. The fourth week you consider the meaning of the Bible. Weeks five and six direct you in two related spiritual practices: prayer and discernment. In week seven you will review Paul's understanding of the church and our role in it. The last two weeks are explorations of our witness: our witness to the God-given gifts of our sexual orientation and our Christian discipleship.

Each day of the week has a devotional exercise. I call them "devotional" because they are designed to both kindle and express your devotion to God in Christ Jesus. I call them "exercises" because they ask more of you than most daily devotions. They ask you to think, to wrestle with difficult or painful issues, to pray, and to consider the scriptures. Each exercise is anchored by and built on a biblical text. Each day you are asked to spend time in prayer. Depending on how deeply you go into the day's topic, you will spend between fifteen minutes to an hour on each exercise.

The Bible and much of the spiritual language of Christianity has been used to vilify and demonize us. If you have been deeply wounded by the church, you may have difficulty picking up a Bible, much less reading it. You may also recoil from some of the language and words I use in these exercises (words like repentance, sacrifice, and obedience). Part of our healing process is to reclaim the Bible and the words—to reclaim them in the context of our lives as lesbian and gay Christians. My hope is that the Spirit will use these exercises to move you through your pain and anger into a fresh encounter with the risen Christ.

I use the New Revised Standard Version (NRSV) of the Bible for scripture passages in this workbook. The NRSV is one of the "formal correspondence translations," those translations that have a more literal word translation and word order. (Other translations in this category include the New King James Version and the New International Version). I use the NRSV because it is the translation widely recognized in ecumenical circles as being the least sectarian of the English translations. However, you will receive a deeper understanding of a particular text by consulting two or three other translations. Each translation discloses a different aspect of the text.

HOW TO USE THIS WORKBOOK

The material in this workbook can bring old emotional issues to the surface. You may find yourself reliving old memories with intense feelings. In this case, you have an opportunity to find peace and God's grace in parts of yourself long tucked away in a closet. Keeping a journal, sharing with friends, and praying about those people and events in your life are all ways of working through these memories and feelings. Some people find therapy with a psychotherapist trained in lesbian and gay issues to be useful in this process.

If you submerge yourself in the Bible study, reflection, and prayer suggested in these pages, you make your-self vulnerable to powerful spiritual forces. Teresa of Avila, the sixteenth-century reformer of the Carmelite order, promised her sisters and brothers: "God withholds himself from no one who perseveres." If you persevere in your quest for God, you will be found by God. Your spiritual life will intensify as you are drawn deeper into your Creator's arms.

Although this resulting emotional and spiritual activity is disruptive to your normal routine, it also makes your life thick with meaning and shapes you in unexpected ways. God is infinitely creative, and we can never foresee how our lives will evolve when our Creator is shaping us. Because the topics in this workbook can elicit such unforeseen intense experiences, you may choose to take longer to work through the devotional exercises than is suggested by its format.

Alternatively, you may decide to stay with the suggested schedule, but go through the workbook more than one time. By staying with the suggested schedule, you get an overview of all aspects of your Christian spiritual-ity during the first reading. Working through the devotional exercises a second time allows you to find the deeper insights you missed during your first exposure to the material.

I published this workbook so that lesbian and gay Christians who are isolated from other gay and lesbian Christians have an opportunity to embark on a structured program of prayer and study. Isolation may be a result of geography or may be a result of a life situation that requires you to live deep in the closet. Whatever the rea-son for your isolation, you can use this workbook alone. You can think about and pray about your sexual orien-tation and your relationship with God in privacy.

Some of you may want to make this journey with other Christians. You can share your journey with others in a variety of formats. You might invite a friend to meet with you every week or every two weeks to pray together, discuss the topics for the week(s) and to reflect on your experiences. In a more formal format, you might gather a group of people to meet weekly for nine weeks, with the workbook creating the agenda for the meetings.

Even those who are isolated in rural areas can gather a "virtual" group. You might create an online group with friends far away, with people you have met in a chat room, or by networking from a website devoted to lesbian and gay Christian concerns. Your group could "meet" through e-mail or in real time in a chat room.

If you do embark on this reconciling journey with others, I suggest you choose one of the group to be your prayer partner. A prayer partner is someone who prays for you and for whom you pray. You will find a suggested prayer for your prayer partner at the beginning of each week.

Some of you may have been given this workbook by your psychotherapist as an adjunct to therapy. Spiritual issues are rooted in emotional issues. An impasse in one area often creates an impasse in the other area. This workbook evolved out of a program that straddled the line between the therapy room and the church. Nonetheless, it is weighted toward more theological and spiritual issues rather than psychological and emotional issues. Consequently, this workbook makes a good complement to psychotherapy.

However you decide to use this workbook, my prayer for you is that your discipleship deepens, your spirituality intensifies, and your life becomes more holy. "May grace and peace be yours in abundance in the knowledge of God and of Jesus our Lord" (2 Pet. 1:2).

Week One   MY FAITH STORY

For many of us who grew up in the church, our spiritual journey began in Sunday School class, or summer camp, or even a tent revival. We first encountered God in our teachers, preachers, and parents. Since those early years, our lives may have led us into unexpected places. This workbook is another episode in our journey. We begin this episode in our journey by reviewing our faith journey.

In the New Testament, the Greek word for the noun "faith" is the same as the verb "believe," Today we tend to equate the act of believing with agreeing to a set of propositions (like the Apostle's Creed, or the "inerrancy of the Bible"). However, the New Testament meaning of belief is a much larger process than something that goes on inside our head. Faith is what we are devoted to; what we rest our heart on; what we spend our lives on; what shapes and organizes our lives as individuals and in community.

Our faith in God creates a relationship with the divine that shapes our lives. We struggle to give words, images, stories, and ideas to that faith. However, none of our finite efforts to capture our relationship with God will ever be complete and sufficient. When we make the mistake of confusing our words *about* God with God, we engage in idolatry. When we worship an institution, a creed, or a set of fundamental beliefs, we no longer worship an infinite God who created us, but a finite human construction.

The history of the Hebrews is a story of a chosen people who are called to worship the one true God. And yet they repeatedly stray into idolatry and worship human-created gods. Despite their infidelity, God welcomes them back and sustains them in a covenant relationship. Today, we continue to be tempted into worshipping a human construction, an idol. But God waits for us to come to our senses and return to worship our Creator.

You have drawn the name of another group member. Start each day's reflection period with a short prayer for that person. You might pray the following:

Thank you, Creator of every life, for _____ *[name]. We rejoice that you have given us fellow pilgrims. Fill our hearts with your love and understanding that we might find wholeness in our faith journey. Amen.*

DAY ONE   ❈   Faith

Hebrews 11 is the great "faith" chapter of the New Testament. The author recounts the deeds of the women and men of faith in Israelite history. Read the introduction in Hebrews 11:1–3. Faith is assurance, conviction, and understanding. Faith is a devotion so intense it shapes all that we do and are. Take a few moments and consider what you set your heart on. To what (or whom) are you devoted?

Read the author's encouraging conclusion in the first two verses of chapter 12. How does Jesus' endurance of the cross and its shame support your faith?

MEDITATION

Close your eyes and imagine the "great cloud of witnesses" surrounding you and supporting you as you "run with perseverance the race that is set before" you.

DAY TWO   ✻   **A Devoted Life**

We have many "idols" in this culture: financial security, status, materialism, religion. *Religion?* Yes, religion. When church and religion have more to do with who is in and who is out, with who is good and who is bad, with a social hierarchy defining our status, then religion becomes an idol, unworthy of our faith. When we worship religion rather than God, we are engaged in idolatry.

Has religion or church ever been an idol for you? How?

In Psalm 51:15–17, the psalmist makes a distinction between a contrite heart willing to heed God's voice, and the ritual sacrifices of the temple. Take a moment to read and ponder this text. How might resting your heart on God be different from devoting yourself to religion or the church?

MEDITATION

Reread the three verses from Psalm 51 several times. Close your eyes and imagine yourself offering to God your willingness to follow God's way for you.

DAY THREE ❋ Mapping Your Spiritual Journey

For the next four days, you will be completing the chart on the next page. It is designed to help you trace patterns and trends in your spiritual journey. This activity is an opportunity to review your life and different stages of faithfulness and awareness. You may wish to duplicate this chart to accommodate all the years of your life.

Today's task is the first three columns. Begin with the year of your birth. Write down your age and where you lived in the next two columns. As you write down each year, allow your mind to wander. Note any memories or thoughts here:

As you remember the places you have lived, do certain sights, sounds, or smells come back to you? What feelings are associated with these memories? Can you detect God's presence?

MEDITATION

Close your eyes, relax, and allow the swirl of memories to flow through your awareness. Some may be painful, some full of joy. Offer them all to God.

YEAR	AGE	LOCATION	WHAT I DID	MAJOR LIFE EVENTS	IMPORTANT RELATIONSHIPS

SIGNIFICANT EVENTS IN THE CULTURE	WHAT I VALUED	MY IMAGES OF GOD	AUTHORITIES

DAY FOUR ❄ The Things I Have Done

Review yesterday's notes. Today you will complete the next two columns. Under "What I did," write down the activities that most absorbed you during that year. It could include school, work, family, friends, or sports. Under "Major life events" write down key personal events: graduation, births and deaths, moves. Note any major event that impacted your life. It does not have to be a "big" event to have had a large impact. For example, some children are significantly affected when their best friend moves away.

As you review the major events in your life, which one(s) do you consider the worst? Why?

Which events do you consider the best, or happiest, events in your life? What about the event made it the best?

MEDITATION

Sit quietly with your eyes closed. Picture the worst and best times in your life. Allow the feelings to come to the surface. Thank God for these times.

DAY FIVE ❋ **My Relationships and My World**

Under "Important relationships," write down the people who were important to you during that time of your life. What relationships have you sustained? What relationships have been broken off or have simply disappeared? Did any relationship have a significant impact on you? If so, how?

The next column is "Significant events in the culture," Under this column write down all those things that provide a cultural context for your life at that time. Those things might include wars, the AIDS epidemic, a recession, even a popular form of entertainment. As you note these dynamics across your lifetime, did any of them change the course of your life? If so, how?

MEDITATION

With your eyes closed and a quiet mind, pray for a person who was once important to you, but who is no longer a part of your life.

DAY SIX　❋　**Sources of Influence**

Today you will complete the chart of your faith journey by filling in the final three columns. Under "What I valued," note what was important to you in this period of your life. What yardstick did you use to evaluate yourself? What shaped your behavior and determined how you saw yourself and others? In school, for example, that yardstick might have been grades, popularity, or athletic ability. Or it might be "holiness" or something like "being cool." It could have been an organization, a group of people, or even ideas.

Under "My images of God," write down how you saw God during this time period. Was God distant? Close? Loving? Punitive? Like your father or mother? Like your pastor?

The final column is labeled "Authorities." Under this column, write down the people, the groups, or the institutions that gave you guidance. Who did you look to for validation of your opinions? For reality testing? For your sense of strength and stability?

After you have completed the last column, spend a few moments reviewing your work. Write down any thoughts that come to you as you review your chart:

MEDITATION

As you meditate on your journey, ask God to show you the Spirit's movement in your life. How and when was God most present? Most absent?

DAY SEVEN ❋ **Reflecting on My Spiritual Journey**

Review your chart. If you were to divide your life into chapters, where would they begin and end? What would be the chapter titles?

Do you see any recurring themes in your life? What are they? How has your faith shaped those themes? How has religion or church shaped (or misshaped) those themes?

MEDITATION

Ask God to open your eyes and give you wisdom and insight into your spiritual path to date. Listen for God's prompting for the present.

We begin to build our ideas about God and our emotional response to God as very young children. Our most powerful experiences are in our relationships with our parents or primary caretakers. We are utterly dependent upon them, and they hold god-like power over us. Our parents are our gods when we are young. The emotional foundation of our experience of God is based on highly variable, early family relationships, with all their potential for brokenness and error.

Out of these early experiences, we may have internalized an image of God that has *more* to do with family, religion, and culture and *less* to do with an authentic relationship with our loving Creator. Sometimes these images merge with biblical images of God to create powerful situations in which family patterns are enacted on a cosmic scale. As lesbian and gay persons, we are particularly vulnerable to destructive parental imagery masquerading in Christian imagery.

We not only confuse authority figures with God, we can also confuse our emotional responses to our parents with our emotional response to God. For example, we may confuse the feeling of safety and contentment that comes with the approval of our parents with the feeling of being loved by God. Conversely, we may confuse our anxiety attendant to "breaking the family rules" with God's displeasure and wrath. Confusing early family feelings and patterns for our status with God may keep us stuck in a disordered relationship with God.

This week we will remember key early experiences that shaped our images of God. We will reflect on biblical images of God and compare those with our inherited images of God. We will learn to pray to the God of the Bible, not the old white guy (with beard) peering down at us from behind a cloud.[1]

Remember to start each day's reflection period with a short prayer for your prayer partner. You could pray the following:

Mother Father God, bless my fellow pilgrim _____ *with your love and wisdom. Be with us as we seek to know your many faces. Amen.*

1. Much of this material is adapted from Dale and Juanita Ryan, Recovery from *Distorted Images of God* (Downers Grove, Ill.: 1990).

DAY ONE ❈ Early Experiences

Examine the following descriptors:

Expects the impossible	Expects the possible
Emotionally distant	Emotionally available
Uninterested	Attentive and involved
Abusive	Healing
Unreliable	Faithful
Abandons you	Reaches out to you

Think of a time when an adult important in your life behaved in one or more ways portrayed by the descriptors in the list above. Describe that event. What was that like for you? How did you feel?

Now recall an incident in your childhood in which an adult's behavior reflected the descriptors from the list on the right. Describe that event. How was that event different from the first incident?

MEDITATION

Close your eyes and allow yourself to remember each incident in turn. Which of the two encounters most reflects your experience of God? Sit with your thoughts and feelings for a few moments and bring them before God. Then ask God to reorder your relationship in the coming weeks.

DAY TWO ✳ **God Has Reasonable Expectations of Us**

God calls us into service and obedience. When we grow up in critical environments, scripture that calls us to obedience may be used by others to revile who we are. Many of us have heard "homosexuality" condemned in church and at home. We may have even spent years praying that God change us. But God has not changed our sexual orientation. Maybe expecting God to change us is not God's desire for us. Maybe expecting a gay or lesbian person to walk in the world as a heterosexual person is unreasonable.

Read Isaiah 45:9–12.

You are the work of God's hands, the clay in the hands of the potter, begotten by the father and brought forth by the mother. What does this scripture say to those who demand that God change your sexual orientation?

What sort of reasonable expectations might God have of you as a lesbian or gay Christian?

MEDITATION

Imagine yourself as clay in God's hands, being molded as a lesbian or gay child of God.

DAY THREE ❋ Immanuel, God with Us

Many of us grew up in a culture that minimizes feelings, especially negative, painful ones. When in pain, we may have been called "cry baby," or "selfish," or told we were feeling sorry for ourselves. All of these messages leave us alone with our more painful feelings. Yet God wants to be with us, even in our darkest moments.

Read Hebrews 4:14–16.

As lesbian and gay Christians struggling to be faithful in a homophobic church, our greatest weakness is the shame we harbor over our sexual orientation. Jesus was also put to shame (Mark 15:16–20), told he was sinful, and called one of the devil's own (Matt. 12:24). How do these experiences make him able to sympathize with our weaknesses?

This scripture claims it is now possible to "approach God with confidence." What might this mean in your life today as a lesbian or gay person?

MEDITATION

Picture yourself approaching God confidently and sharing your shameful feelings about being gay. Hear God say, "Receive my mercy. Here is grace for you in your time of need."

DAY FOUR ❋ **God Attends To Us**

Church leaders, teachers, and parents may have repeatedly told us how God attends to us and knows "every hair on our head." Yet we are apt to hear the message that God is only attentive to "good people"—not gay and lesbian persons. We feel attended to only when we ignore that aspect of ourselves. When we embrace our sexuality, we may experience God as turning from us.

Do you assume that God has turned from you as a lesbian or gay person? What is that like?

Stand in front of a mirror and read Psalm 139:1–18 aloud to yourself.

Verse 16b says "In your book were written all the days that were formed for me, when none of them as yet existed."

The days God formed for you are days as a lesbian or gay person. Reread this section aloud, keeping this thought in mind. God knew (and treasured) your sexual orientation before you were born. What is your experience when hearing these words?

MEDITATION

The author says to God "your hand shall lead me and your right hand shall hold me fast." After spending a few moments in silence, picture in your mind God's hands leading you and "holding you fast."

DAY FIVE ✳ **God Heals**

Many of us experience physical, emotional, and/or verbal abuse about being lesbian or gay Christians. We may then translate that experience emotionally as God being abusive and willing to hurt us. Yet the God of the Bible is one who heals us of our brokenness and is ready to act for us in spite of cultural constraints.

Read Mark 3:1–6.

The man with the withered hand was huddled in the synagogue, just as we huddle in a hostile church. In the midst of a hostile environment, Jesus brings God's healing presence. What do you think the man thought and felt when he saw Jesus approach him? As Jesus healed him?

Our anxiety, shame, and sense of inferiority due to our sexual orientation are as crippling as this man's hand. Where are you huddled? How does Jesus find you and heal you?

MEDITATION

Reread today's scripture, but replace the man with the withered hand with yourself. Imagine Jesus calling you into relationship and healing you of your sense of shame.

DAY SIX ✻ God Is Faithful

Even those of us with reliable, loving parents may believe that they would not love us if we are "bad" (or gay or lesbian). We may translate this experience into an image of God as being unreliable, as loving us only when we are "good" (i.e., not gay). We may think that we can no longer count on God's presence if we allow ourselves to embrace our sexual orientation. Yet the Bible names God the Faithful One, the Rock, the Fortress. Our family may desert us when they discover our sexual orientation. Our friends may shun us when they learn we are gay. Our boss may fire us and our churches condemn us. But God is faithful, our Rock and Redeemer.

Read Psalm 145:8–21.

Write the phrases that suggest God is reliable and faithfully present:

Change verse 9 as indicated, then read verses 8 and 9 aloud:

"The Lord is gracious and merciful,

   slow to anger and abounding in steadfast love.

The Lord is good to _____ [*your name*],

   and his compassion is over me and all that he has made."

What images, thoughts, feelings, etc. come to you as you reflect on this exercise?

MEDITATION

"The Lord is near to all who call on him." Picture yourself at a Pride parade and call on God. Ask God to draw near to you.

DAY SEVEN ✸ **God Initiates Relationship**

As children, we may have experienced abandonment through death, divorce, desertion, parental workaholism, or the illness of a parent. As we come out to those around us, we experience that abandonment all over again. Out of these traumatic experiences, we can develop an image of God who will abandon us. To make matters worse, we have been told that God will abandon us if we accept ourselves as lesbian or gay persons. Others tell us that *we* abandon *God* if we accept ourselves as whole, gay Christians. But the God of the Bible is not a God that abandons.

    Read Matthew 18:10–14.

    Although other Christians may drive us away from the fold by condemning our sexual orientation, the Good Shepherd treasures us so much he leaves all the others behind in order to bring us home to him. As a lesbian or gay Christian, have you ever felt like a sheep lost in the hills? What is that experience like for you?

    Some of us have been so shamed and belittled, we "lose God" when we come out. What comes to mind when you picture God looking for you as diligently as the shepherd in the parable searches for the lost sheep?

MEDITATION

Imagine yourself lost in a wilderness of shame, loneliness, and confusion as a lesbian or gay person. Suddenly the Good Shepherd appears, embraces you, and brings you home.

Being gay or lesbian in a homophobic culture makes our relationships with others, with ourselves, and with God difficult. In order to survive, we sometimes hide our sexual orientation, bringing only a part of ourselves into relationships. Some of us even lie to friends and family. We might change the pronouns when talking about our activities over the weekend, evade questions about dating, or put the picture of an opposite-sex friend on our desk at work. In an effort to be the straight person the world wants us to be, we live a lie.

Living in a hostile culture has multiple costs: financial, emotional, social, and physical. Sometimes we numb ourselves to the emotional fallout with drugs and alcohol, indiscriminate sex, or materialism. We develop bad habits that disorder our relationships with ourselves, with God, and with others in our community.

God calls each of us into discipleship and some form of Christian service. But we cannot imagine God using us. We are like the two sons in Matthew 21:28. Some of us refuse to work in our Father's vineyard, sure that we are too flawed to be of service. Others of us are like the other son. We tell our Father we will go and work in the vineyard, but lose our heart for service when we discover we belong to a group of people despised and rejected by the very people we are called to serve. In either case, we allow the pain of being a gay or lesbian Christian to seduce us into disobedience. Our relationship with God is disordered.

The life, death, and resurrection of Jesus create a way for us to be reconciled: with ourselves, with others, and with God. In Jesus, we find our way back to God. In Jesus, we find a companion and fellow traveler, someone who knows suffering, condemnation by the religious establishment, and crucifixion.

Remember to start each day's reflection period with a short prayer for your prayer partner. You could pray the following:

Precious Savior, pour your blessings on my sister/brother in Christ, _____ . *Holy One who has emptied his life for us, forgive us our sin and show us your salvation. Amen.*

DAY ONE   ✳   **The Betrayed Christ**

In the gospel of Mark, Jesus told his disciples: "'The Son of Man is to be betrayed into human hands, and they will kill him, and three days after being killed, he will rise again.' But they did not understand what he was saying and were afraid to ask him" (Mark 9:31–32).

The disciples did not understand what Jesus was talking about. But Jesus knew that a trusted friend, a person who worshipped with him, prayed with him, and broke bread with him, would betray him. And he knew that the leaders of his own church would have him killed. What do you think it was like for him to know that a person close to him would betray him? That his betrayal would end in crucifixion?

Have you ever been betrayed? By a person? By your church? What was that experience like for you?

MEDITATION

Close your eyes and let your mind become quiet. Picture a particularly painful moment of betrayal. Ask Jesus to stand by you.

DAY TWO ❋ **Sin**

Too many times, we are told our sexual orientation is a sin, or that our most loving relationships are an abomination in the eyes of God. We may respond to these messages with an abiding sense of being stained, marked by a character defect exclusive to our kind and ourselves. Others of us respond by rejecting the notion of sin altogether.

Yet Paul tells us: *"For there is no distinction, since all have sinned and fall short of the glory of God"* (Rom. 3:22b–23). We bear the burden of others' sin against us, and we ourselves sin against others and against God. We cease to be victims and become whole, grounded persons when we accept responsibility for our sin. This means we do *not* seek forgiveness for those "sins" resulting from oppression (that is, our sexual orientation, our shame), and *do* accept responsibility for the *real* sin in our lives (such as managing our shame with alcohol, trying to be the person others want us to be). Make two columns. In one column, write down what others say are your sins. In the other column, write down your real sins, those areas of willfulness that interfere with your relationship with God and with others.

What others say are my sins	My real sins

As you think about your two lists, do you see patterns? Do you see a relationship between the two lists? To what extent does your sin grow out of areas of shame and brokenness?

MEDITATION

Spend some time in silence, waiting for God's presence. Bring your two lists to God and ask for wisdom and guidance.

DAY THREE ❈ **Confession**

"Christ Jesus our Lord, in whom we have access to God in boldness and confidence through faith in him" (Eph. 3:11b, 12).

When we identify areas of sin in our lives, we accept responsibility for our lives. But admitting that we have sinned can be difficult. We might feel embarrassed, ashamed, or guilty over some of the things we have done with our lives. Those bad feelings threaten to come to the surface if we even think about those things, much less say them out loud. What bad feelings do you have when you think of particular sins in your life?

Despite the anxiety we might feel, as Christians we know that we can acknowledge our sin with the confidence that we are understood, loved, and forgiven. Write a letter to God in which you tell God of your sins. Either use the space below, or write your letter on a separate sheet of paper.

MEDITATION

Bring your confession to God by reading your letter out loud. Ask for forgiveness. Sometimes it is helpful to share difficult secrets with another Christian. If you think it would be helpful, share your letter with a trusted friend, pastor, mentor, or lover.

DAY FOUR   ❀   **Grace and Forgiveness**

Read Luke 15:11–32.

   Verse 17 tells us that the prodigal son "came to himself." What do you think it was like for the son to come to himself? Have you ever had that experience? What happened? How did you feel when you came to yourself?

   The prodigal son expected his father to take him back as a hired hand. Yet his father received him as his son. In the same way, when we confess our sin before our Creator, we are restored into a right relationship with God. Our shame and guilt are replaced by a cleansing contrition—a sense of profound sorrow mixed with deep gratitude and a sweet peace of basking in God's love. When was the last time you were touched by God's grace? How would you describe your experience?

MEDITATION

Allow your God-inspired gratitude to come to the surface of your awareness. Spend a few moments praising God for God's graciousness.

DAY FIVE　❋　**Forgiving Others**

Scripture repeatedly tells us of the reciprocal relationship between receiving and giving forgiveness (see, for example, Luke 11:4 and Matt. 18:21–35). Sometimes these passages are used to encourage people to forgive persecutors, oppressors, and other hurtful people before the injured one is ready to forgive them. Have you ever had this experience? If so, what was the result of forced, premature forgiveness?

Although premature forgiveness is destructive, we do not want to go through life dragging a burden of anger and resentment. Praying certain Psalms can help us put our anger and pain into words. Eventually, we can learn to leave our anger and pain in God's hands. Do you harbor an old grudge or resentment? Write about it in the space below. Then read Psalm 94 out loud.

MEDITATION

Ultimately, only God can transform our resentment into forgiveness—yet another act of grace. Ask God to soften your heart anger and give you a forgiving heart.

DAY SIX　❋　**The Crucified Christ**

The early church recognized the work of Jesus in the four Servant of Yahweh poems found in Isaiah (42:1–4, 49:1–6, 50:4–9, 52:13–53:12). Through the suffering of the Servant, God inaugurates the realm of God. In the intervening two thousand years, multiple models have been proposed to "explain" this mystery of God's redemption.

One model of Jesus as the suffering Servant is that of scapegoat, the One who carries the sins of the world. This model is derived from a primitive ritual in which members of a small clan selected a goat on which to heap all their sin and shame. The goat was then driven out of the village and into the desert, carrying away the sins of the people.

In our current culture, many people project their own sense of shame and guilt onto lesbian and gay persons. We then get stoned, driven into the desert, or crucified. Read Isaiah 52:13–53:12. Do you find any similarities between the fate of the Man of Sorrows and events in your own life? If so, what are they?

Although Jesus was the victim of the times and the crowd's prejudice and fears, God transformed his suffering and death into life for the very people who betrayed and crucified him. How might your life be different if you were to identify your experience of persecution as a lesbian or gay Christian as a way of being crucified with Christ?

MEDITATION

Find a crucifix or a picture of one. Spend some time meditating on Jesus' shame and suffering during that ordeal. Then imagine that you join him on the cross. Bring him your hurts and suffering.

DAY SEVEN ❋ **The Resurrected Christ**

In an unexpected reversal, God created life out of the suffering and death of Jesus. Read Romans 8:31–39. In this passage, Paul promises us that only Christ Jesus can "bring any charge against God's elect," and that nothing will separate us from the love of God in Christ Jesus. Verse 34 assures us that only Jesus can judge us—not our parents or our pastor or our Sunday school teacher. As children of God, as God's elect, we can be confident of God's love in Christ Jesus.

How would your relationships change if you believed Paul's words applied to you? What would be different in your daily life?

We can become stuck in our despair about our lives as lesbian and gay persons in a homophobic church. Or we can work through our despair and live a resurrected life. Paul promises "in all these things we are more than conquerors through him who loved us," Christ's love for us can overcome all obstacles, even homophobia. Can you believe this? How have you experienced Christ's love overcoming other obstacles in your life?

MEDITATION
Reread today's scripture. Ask God to convince you that you are "more than [a] conqueror[s] through him who loved us."

Week Four

THE INSPIRED AND INSPIRING WORD OF GOD[2]

For many of us, the Bible is a land mine. We are drawn to the scriptures in order to encounter God and to hear the word of God for our lives. And yet the Bible is used to demean us and to tell us that God hates us. Many Christians tell us that "the Bible says" we are hateful to God, an abomination to God, or that our loving relationships are "incompatible with the gospel."

The Bible is full of inconsistencies, self-contradictions, and even self-corrections. Sometimes specific details contradict each other. For example, Paul gives instruction on how women are to pray and prophesy in church in 1 Corinthians 11:5 but 1 Corinthians 14:34 tells women to be silent in church.

The Bible is also inconsistent by presenting particular narratives that contradict broader biblical principles. For example, themes of grace, justice, and a unity in Christ that knows no distinction (Gal. 3:28) are contradicted by stories that condone slavery (Philemon), the submission of women to men, and death as punishment for lying to the church (Acts 5:1–11).

We don't like inconsistencies and ambiguity. We sometimes try to erase these inconsistencies by providing arguments that present only one side as the "truth." Because of our tendency towards self-deception (a part of our fallen state), our attempts to harmonize scripture reflect our prejudice. We are likely to emphasize the side of an issue that reinforces our own view of the world and force conflicting material into that interpretation.

Many Christians who advocate a "literal" interpretation of the Bible choose certain texts to condemn us and ignore or explain away conflicting texts. Other Christians investigate authorship, sources, and editorial activities (called historical criticism) to account for inconsistencies in scripture. Although this approach provides a base of objectivity on one level, on another level, how we interpret our findings reflects our own perspective of the world.

For this reason, we are *all* called to a confessional approach to Bible study. We come to scripture and ask the Spirit of Christ to reveal God's truth to us, confessing our own bias. As with all spiritual disciplines, this is a difficult practice and requires letting go of our preconceived ideas. If we are to catch a glimpse of God's view of the world, we must learn to relinquish our own.

Remember to start each day's reflection period with a short prayer for your prayer partner. You could pray the following:

Thank you, Author of our lives, for your creation of _____ . *I treasure my fellow pilgrim as a gift from you. May your Spirit enlighten our encounters with your Word. Amen.*

2. See the appendix for a more thorough treatment of biblical interpretation.

DAY ONE ❊ The Inspiring Word

"How sweet are your words to my taste, sweeter than honey to my mouth!" (Ps. 119:103).

When we come to scripture with our hearts first and our heads second, we come to be infused with the Holy Spirit. We find in scripture a manifestation of God that encourages, informs, illuminates, and guides. Many times when we come to Bible study, we come looking for an encounter with God. Over time, our lives are shaped and formed by God in the Word of God.

Different parts of the Bible inspire us at different times in our lives. At any given time, we may find one verse or passage especially compelling and influential. In the same way, certain texts may be compelling for a given church during a particular time in the life of that church. Having different texts speak to us at different times is part of the dynamic nature of the Word. Have you had the experience of the words of God being "sweeter than honey to my mouth"? Which words? How did those words illumine your relationship with God?

Because we find certain texts compelling, we are at risk of distorting the meaning of those texts by reading them out of context and without regard for the larger Bible. Because we are most vulnerable to the distorting influence of sin when we are being drawn closer to God, those compelling texts can become destructive. Has that ever happened in your life? In a church of which you were a member? What could you do to test your reading of the scripture? How would you discern distortion?

MEDITATION

Thank God for making God's words sweeter than honey in your mouth. Ask God to inspire your Bible reading as you seek God's words to you this week.

DAY TWO ❧ **The Inspired Word**

"All scripture is inspired by God" (2 Tim. 3:16a).

Although our faith tradition assumes the Bible is the inspired word of God, we don't agree on what "inspired by God" means. For some, inspired means that God has seen to it that every word and concept in the Bible is true in the way they think of truth. The problem with this view is that it ignores biblical inconsistencies and limits "truth" to something that can be understood by human minds. Other Christians assert that the divine inspiration of the Bible means that it cannot be analyzed and studied the way other texts are studied. This approach rejects any attempt to bring contemporary research methods to the study of the Bible.

Another way of understanding inspiration is that over time the church has recognized this group of writings as manifesting the Spirit of God in our faith community. Although we cannot account for the actual workings of the original inspiration, we continue to witness the grace that scripture brings to the church. Do you think the Bible is inspired by God? If so, what do you think that means?

Technically, a text that is "inspired" is "in-Spirited." Just as we were created with God's breath, the scriptures were created by God breathing God's Spirit into them. Does the inspired nature of scripture limit how we study it? Should we only read and pray the text? Or should we only study results of scholarly research? How are we called to approach scripture that is inspired and inspiring?

MEDITATION

Ask God to teach you how to study God's scriptures.

DAY THREE ❈ **The Function of Scripture**

"All scripture is inspired by God and is useful for teaching, for reproof, for correction, and for training in right-eousness, so that everyone who belongs to God may be proficient, equipped for every good work" (2 Tim. 3:16–17).

Many of us from "Bible-based" faith traditions have heard this text from our childhood. It is used to make the Bible's primary function be a guide for righteousness with a code of right thinking and of right conduct. With this foundation, a systematic code of ethics and set of dogmatic propositions are then used as yardsticks to evaluate the faithfulness of persons and churches. For these Christians, failure in either conduct or belief results in a fall from grace.

In your faith tradition, what was the Bible's primary function? Did your tradition emphasize a code of conduct or a set of beliefs that were then "proven" with texts from the Bible? What were those codes? How were they reinforced? How was the Bible used in that process?

The problem with this approach is that the core element of Christianity is Jesus Christ, not a code of ethics or a philosophical system. How can our approach to scripture reflect our conviction that the life, death, and resurrection of Christ is the crux of our religion? How do ethics and belief fit into that approach?

MEDITATION

"And the Word became flesh and lived among us, and we have seen his glory, the glory as of a father's only son, full of grace and truth" (John 1:14). When you have memorized this scripture, spend a few moments praying it.

DAY FOUR ✳ **The Killing Letter and the Life-Giving Spirit**

In 2 Corinthians, Paul explains the basis of his ministry, saying: "Our competence is from God, who has made us competent to be ministers of a new covenant, not of letter but of spirit; for the letter kills, but the Spirit gives life" (2 Cor. 3:5b–6). He is claiming the Spirit of Christ as the formational force in his life as an apostle, not the Mosaic letter of the law.

We are as guilty of clinging to the letter of the law today as the Christians were in Corinth. One way we cling to the letter of the law is to lift a sentence out of the Bible and use it as our sole guideline for behavior in a certain area. Conservative Christians are more likely to make this mistake. Another way we cling to the letter that kills is to let the results of historical criticism give us the final meaning of a text. Liberal Christians are more likely to make this mistake.

Have you been among church groups who cling to the letter? How? What were the consequences?

In the introduction, we saw that using historical critical methods helps avoid the distortion that occurs when we take a biblical text out of context. However, when we use the results of historical criticism to define the text, we create a new distortion. We freeze scripture into one meaning. How might the Spirit form us through Bible study based in historical critical methods? How is prayer a part of this process?

MEDITATION

Spend a few moments thanking God for the gift of God's Word. Ask God to send the life-giving Spirit into your Bible study.

DAY FIVE ❈ Sodom and Gomorrah

Within recent history of western Christianity, people who engage in same-sex behavior have been called Sodomites. This term comes from a city destroyed by God for its sin. Read the precipitating event of God's destruction of Sodom and Gomorrah in Genesis 19:1–11. The crowd of men outside of Lot's door wants to humiliate Lot's guests by raping them. This practice was a way of establishing dominance by hostile enemies or conquering armies during that time. (This information is an example of using historical critical scholarship to understand scripture.)

At first glance, we might think rape is the sin that kindles God's wrath against Sodom. Then we notice Lot's first attempted solution. He says to the crowd: "Look, I have two daughters who have not known a man; let me bring them out to you, and do to them as you please" (Gen. 19:8a). Apparently, Lot preferred his virgin daughters to be raped by all the men in town rather than give up the strangers to the horde outside his door. What do you think motivated Lot to make such a response? What does Lot's offer suggest about how he values his daughters? Of women in general? Of family relationships?

Obviously sex, even the rape of Lot's daughters, is not the sin in this story. In another Old Testament text, God says: "This was the guilt of your sister Sodom: she and her daughters had pride, excess of food, and prosperous ease, but did not aid the poor and needy" (Ezek. 16:49). When Jesus sent his disciples on a mission he told them to leave those who did not welcome them. He said: "Truly I tell you, it will be more tolerable for the land of Sodom and Gomorrah on the day of judgment than for that town" (Matt. 10:1–15). Given these texts, what do you think is the sin of Sodom and Gomorrah? Why?

MEDITATION

Pray over this story and ask God for God's wisdom to illuminate its truth.

DAY SIX ❋ **Romans**

The first three chapters of Romans are an extended argument that supports Paul's conclusion that "there is no distinction: since all have sinned and fall short of the glory of God" (Rom. 3:23). Paul is demonstrating that Jews, despite being chosen by God, are no less sinful than Gentiles. He does this by listing the sinfulness of the Gentiles in chapter 1 and of the Jews in chapter 2.

In describing the sinfulness of the Gentiles, Paul says that although God is manifested in creation, the Gentiles preferred to worship the created, not the Creator. The Gentiles were guilty of idolatry. Because they committed idolatry, Paul says that God "gave them up to degrading passions" (see Rom. 1:26–27). In other words, Paul's "degrading passions" are the *results* of the sin of idolatry. Using his logic, everyone who commits idolatry should have a same-sex orientation. Remember when you first realized you were attracted to someone of the same sex. Were you any more idolatrous than your straight friends?

Paul demonstrated the consequences of Gentile idolatry by using a science lesson of his day. Today we know that sexual orientation is inborn. Our attraction to someone of the same sex is not the consequence of our idolatry, but is the result of our genetic heritage. If Paul were making the same argument today, he might use a different example of the consequences of idolatry. If he were writing today, what other examples could he use to demonstrate the consequences of idolatry?

MEDITATION

Today pray about these ironies: The story denouncing the inhospitality of Sodom is used to reject lesbian and gay persons from the church. Paul's argument against self-righteous judgment by Jewish Christians of Gentile Christians is used by straight Christians to condemn lesbian and gay Christians.

DAY SEVEN ❋ **Does Paul Have Something to Say to Us?**

In the last two Bible studies, we began to see the many different messages the Bible has about sex and about family relationships. Lot offered his daughters for gang rape. Paul used a now-outdated science lesson to illustrate the consequences of idolatry. A comprehensive study of the Bible will generate a bewildering confusion of exhortations and attitudes toward sex and family structures. Does Paul have anything to say about what to do with our sexual attraction?

In the seventh chapter of 1 Corinthians, Paul is responding to a question about celibacy. Some in the church are teaching that even married persons are to refrain from sex. Read this chapter now. Although Paul prefers they be unencumbered with the demands of a spouse, he suggests that they are better off to marry than to burn with lust. Paul tells both wives and husbands to not deprive the other of their bodies "so that Satan may not tempt you because of your lack of self-control" (1 Cor. 7:5). Lust is an opportunity for Satan to become active. Paul says the primary point of marriage is to provide a safe outlet for the lust of both wife and husband. How does this characterization of marriage differ from what you were taught in church?

In this chapter, Paul makes a strong argument about how married life distracts from service to God (1 Cor. 7:32–35). But if sexual passion is too intense to control, Paul concedes that marriage is no sin. Yesterday, we saw that Paul's understanding of the origin of same-sex attraction was based on an outdated science lesson. If Paul had our current understanding of sexual orientation and attraction, how do you think he would advise lesbian and gay Christians to manage lust?

MEDITATION

Bring this understanding of the relationship between sexual passion and marriage to God in prayer. Ask God for guidance of your sexual activity in your life.

MAKING OURSELVES AVAILABLE TO GOD

We find God by looking deep within ourselves, not by looking "out there." God's presence resides within us: a quiet voice hard to hear in the clatter and clamor of our thoughts and feelings. The biggest obstacle to hearing God's voice is what some spiritual writers call the false self.

We are bombarded with messages every day—messages about us, others, values, and worthiness. We begin absorbing these messages as young children and become increasingly unconscious of them as we mature. Old feelings of shame, guilt, or fear can accompany messages like "I'm no good unless I am perfect" or "I'm a sinful person when I enjoy sex." Because we are not welcome in most churches, a particularly painful message for lesbian and gay Christians is "Life outside of the church is not worth living."

Some messages talk of conditions we must meet in order to be worthy of love. For example, one message might be "I'm a good person as long as I pay my bills on time" or "I'm okay as long as everyone likes me." Feelings of satisfaction, worthiness, and contentment can accompany these messages as long as we satisfy those conditions.

All of these messages make up an image of ourselves that we think we ought to be. Too often, this image is the false self created by the expectations of those around us, not the person God created us to be. Our challenge is to become aware of our self-talk, to identify the resulting image of ourselves, and to learn to turn that image over to God.

When we pray, we make ourselves vulnerable to God: to God's guidance, to God's love, to God's chastisement, to God's grace, to God's forgiveness, to God's healing, to God's challenge. In an ongoing process of formation, God chips away at our false self, molding us and guiding us into authentic Christian living. Sometimes our formation is painful, sometimes exhilarating. This week we will identify some aspects of our "false self" and learn to hear God's voice within us.

Remember to start each day's reflection period with a short prayer for your prayer partner. You could pray the following:

God with us, bless the life of _____ . *Let my fellow pilgrim know the challenge and comfort of your loving presence. May we be forever mindful of your care in the world. Amen.*

DAY ONE ✿ Becoming Aware

Jesus promises, "Ask, and it will be given you; search, and you will find; knock, and the door will be opened for you" (Matt. 7:7). Begin your search for authenticity by becoming aware of messages you heard as a child from family members, church leaders, or friends. What was valued by your family? By your church? By your friends?

    Write the messages you carry around today about the conditions you and others must meet to be worthy of love and respect.

    Thinking about these messages, what is your image of who you *should* be? How is that image different from who you *are*?

Who I should be	Who I really am

MEDITATION

Close your eyes and allow your mind to become quiet. Let your thoughts dwell on your images of who you are and who you think you should be. Ask God to detach you from the images of who you think you should be.

DAY TWO　✳　## Willingness to Be Loved

One of our most significant spiritual challenges is accepting God's unconditional love for us. Lesbian and gay Christians have particular difficulty in acknowledging that we are God's beloved.

Because many of us are afraid that others will reject us if they discover our sexual orientation, we spend a lot of energy "managing" how others perceive us. Fearing that some detail of our life will expose us as gay or lesbian, we control what others know of us. Loss of control over what people know of us is particularly scary for lesbian and gay Christians. Many of us have had to hide our sexual orientation in order to stay in relationship with the church.

We are tempted to bring that control into our relationship with God, to "manage" how God sees us by bringing only a limited part of ourselves before God in prayer. We are afraid to bring our true and full selves before God. We can't imagine how God can love our "real selves."

Do you believe that you must do certain things in order to be beloved of God? What are those things?

What are some of your fears if you were to stop trying to control God's regard and love of you?

MEDITATION

Memorize the following passage. "As the Father has loved me, so I have loved you; abide in my love" (John 15:9). Relax, close your eyes, and imagine Jesus saying these words to you as he holds you in his arms.

DAY THREE ❋ Sacrifice

Even though Jesus tells us that "No one is good but God alone" (Mark 10:18b), we may think we have to "be good" before we can know God in prayer. We may think we are called to sacrifice our power and status, our material possessions, or other ego needs in order to be worthy of God. Yet the spiritual life works the opposite way. As we come to know God in prayer, and as we live in God's grace and love, we begin to embody something of God's goodness.

Paradoxically, what many of us are called to sacrifice is the image of ourselves as "being good." Since we can never "be good," we may feel guilty, ashamed, and inadequate over our pride or greed or lust. Humility is getting beyond our perfectionism and learning to see ourselves realistically. When we come to God, we acknowledge our shortcomings but do not dwell on them or agonize over them. We learn to trust in God's goodness, not our own. Do you think you have to "be good" in order to come to God? What does "being good" mean to you? How do you fail at "being good"?

Close your eyes and see yourself behaving in ways that reflect your failure to "be good." Notice any feelings you may have as you watch yourself. Do not try to stop your thoughts and feelings, just allow them to wash over you and pass away. What do you learn from this exercise?

MEDITATION

Relax, close your eyes, and let your mind become quiet. When you have entered into prayer, ask God to liberate you from perfectionism and teach you humility.

DAY FOUR　❈　**The Discipline of Prayer**

For some of us, developing a prayer life is another "should." We may have learned a message like "A good Christian should spend at least fifteen minutes a day in prayer." In this case, the discipline of prayer is generated from an outside authority, not our own desire for intimacy with God. When we don't pray according to what we "should" pray, then we feel guilty. We think we have not fulfilled our obligation to God.

What "should" messages about prayer do you have? Where and how did you get them?

We cultivate other disciplines out of intense desire. We may spend hours practicing a backhand in tennis. Or we may spend years preparing for a career. All of the disciplined areas of our lives spring from a deep-seated desire. In like manner, we cultivate the discipline of prayer out of a profound longing to know God.

"O God, you are my God, I seek you, my soul thirsts for you; . . . as in a dry and weary land where there is no water" (Ps. 63:1). Remember a time when your soul thirsted for God. When was that? How would you describe that longing?

MEDITATION

Spend a few quiet moments with your eyes closed. Ask God to free you from all the "should" messages that constrict your approach to prayer. Ask God to lead you into an active prayer life.

DAY FIVE ❅ Prayerful Breathing

Breath is a central component of prayer. Sit relaxed in a chair with your eyes closed. Pay attention to your body. Breathe in deeply through your nose and hold it. Then slowly let the air out through your mouth, the tip of your tongue behind your top front teeth. Do this several times. Notice how the tension level in different parts of your body shifts as you breathe in and out. What else do you notice?

The Hebrew word *ruach* is translated as "wind," "breath," or "spirit." The author of Genesis used this word to describe God's breathing the breath of life into all living beings. With each breath we take, we share in God's creating *ruach*. Close your eyes and attend to your breathing. As you breathe in, imagine yourself inhaling God's love. As you breath out, exhale feelings of shame and unworthiness. When you have finished this exercise, write down your thoughts and feelings.

MEDITATION

Close your eyes, relax, and attend to your breathing. As you attend to your breathing, let your mind dwell on these words: "I will cause breath to enter you, and you shall live" (Ez. 37:5b).

DAY SIX ✻ Praying from the Heart

When we pray from the heart, our longing for God leads us into a wordless contemplation. In the Christian tradition, our heart is the seat of our will, our desire, and our deepest yearning. We set our hearts on our longing for and love of God. Our prayer comes from a place beyond words.

"As a deer longs for flowing streams, so my soul longs for you, O God" (Ps. 42:1). Read this sentence until you can remember it. Then relax, focus on your breathing until your mind is quiet, and ponder the words of the psalmist. Allow yourself sufficient time. When you are finished, write down some of your thoughts and feelings.

Some people find it helpful to contemplate a picture as a way of entering into praying from the heart. Find an image that you find compelling—some scene from the life of Jesus that speaks to you. Many people find a scene from the Passion narrative to be particularly gripping. When you have chosen a picture, spend some time looking at it with a quiet mind and relaxed body. You may find you want to close your eyes at some point, or you may prefer to look at the picture throughout your prayer. When you have finished, record your response to this exercise here:

MEDITATION

Pray with neither words nor images. Relax, shut your eyes, and focus on your breathing. Let your awareness expand to your whole body. Finally, bring your awareness into your heart area. Attend to your longing for God.

DAY SEVEN ❄ **When God Prays through Us**

"Likewise the Spirit helps us in our weakness; for we do not know how to pray as we ought, but that very Spirit intercedes [for us] with sighs too deep for words" (Rom. 8:26). Sometimes we do not know how to pray. We may be faced with a problem so complicated, we are not sure what a solution looks like. Other times our pain is buried so deeply, we are not aware of what we need. On yet other occasions, the Spirit of Christ may pray through us for a person or situation we may not even know.

Have you ever had this type of prayer experience? When? What was it like for you?

In the next verse, Paul writes, "And God, who searches the heart, knows what is the mind of the Spirit, because the Spirit intercedes for the saints according to the will of God" (Rom. 8:27). Have you ever had the experience of God searching your heart? Write down some images, adjectives, thoughts, or feelings of that intimate touch. If you have never had that experience, what do you imagine it would be like?

MEDITATION

In your prayer today, ask the Spirit of Christ to invade your heart and your will with that of God's. After making yourself available to God, spend some time in wordless prayer.

*A*s we begin to accept ourselves as lesbian and gay Christians, we wonder why God made us this way. Why did God give us a sexual orientation that marks us as outcasts for most of Christianity? Why do our lives have to be so difficult? What does God want from us?

Although the answers to these questions will vary from individual to individual, we all may reap the benefits of being members of a persecuted group. The psalmist says "The Lord is a stronghold for the oppressed, a stronghold in times of trouble" (Ps. 9:9). Throughout the Bible, God is on the side of those who are marginal: the outcast, the poor, and the oppressed. As we grow in our faith, we learn to detect God's particular presence among us and to take refuge in our Creator rather than to feel sorry for ourselves.

In addition to learning to detect God's presence, times of trial help us learn to discern the promptings of the Spirit and align our will with God's will. The popular cultural myth is that difficulties make us stronger. For the Christian, however, difficult times help us know our limits and brokenness. And in knowing those limits, we learn to rely on God's boundless strength rather than our own finite strength. We learn that our weakness provides more room for God's grace.

We also learn that God's way for our lives is more satisfying than going our own way. God's way is most satisfying because our Creator made us with a deep longing for that way. Obedience to God's will is another way of talking about becoming the authentic lesbian and gay persons God created us to be. Although we are distracted by values and goals from the false self, our only genuine contentment comes from aligning our will with that of God.

But how do we know God's way for our lives? How do we discern the promptings of the Spirit? There is no "surefire" technique or method for knowing God's way. As we live in awareness of God's presence, we become more adept at discerning the Spirit's guidance. This week we will consider different aspects of discerning the Spirit's nurture and guidance.

Remember to start each day's reflection period with a short prayer for your prayer partner. You could pray the following:

Thank you, God of eternal light, for _____ . Bless each of us with the love that illumines all paths. Amen.

DAY ONE ❈ **God's Desire for You**

We may hear discussion of God's will as authoritarian, as violating our autonomy and capacity to choose for ourselves. We may think of God as a distant dictator who burdens us with a direction contrary to our own desire. But God created you and loves you. Within this intimate relationship between you and your Creator, God longs for your life to have a certain shape. God yearns that you be a particular embodiment and expression of the realm of God. And the particular embodiment that God wants for you is rooted in God's creation of you.

Jesus says, "Is there anyone among you who, if your child asks for bread, will give a stone? Or if the child asks for a fish, will give a snake? If you then, who are evil, know how to give good gifts to your children, how much more will your Father in heaven give good things to those who ask him!" (Matt. 7:9–11). Do you have trouble believing that God wants good things for your life? If so, what makes it difficult for you to think God wants good things for you? What would it be like to believe that God wants good things for you?

Close your eyes and imagine yourself standing before God as a gay or lesbian person. Now imagine God *willing* and *longing* for certain things to happen in your life. Take your time and allow the scenario to unfold as it will. When you finish the exercise, write down any thoughts, feelings, or images:

MEDITATION
Ask God to teach you how to discern God's longing for you this week.

DAY TWO ❀ **Our Deepest Desire**

God gave us our temperament, our intelligence, our bodies. God gave us our heart and knows our heart. The psalmist tells us that God knows us inside and out:

> *O Lord, you have searched me and known me,*
> *You know when I sit down and when I rise up;*
> *you discern my thoughts from far away.*
> *You search out my path and my lying down,*
> *and are acquainted with all my ways.*
> *Even before a word is on my tongue,*
> *O Lord, you know it completely. (Ps. 139:1–4)*

God knows the deepest longings of our hearts, many times better than we do. What is your deepest yearning? What does your heart long for?

God's will for us intersects with our deepest, heartfelt desire. God created us, knows us, and wills for us to receive our deepest heart desire. Close your eyes and spend a few moments imagining God yearning for your deepest desire. How does this shape your understanding of God's will for your life? Of your deepest desire for your life?

MEDITATION

During today's prayer time, ask God to help you know your deepest yearnings.

DAY THREE ❋ Accepting All of God's Gifts

"Rejoice always, pray without ceasing, give thanks in all circumstances; for this is the will of God in Christ Jesus for you" (1 Thess. 5:16–18).

Sexual orientation is a gift from God. It is God's will that we be attracted to persons of the same sex. But this precious gift marks us as the modern day equivalent of the unclean. If we take Paul's exhortation seriously, we are to "give thanks in all circumstances" and rejoice that God created us gay or lesbian persons. Until we learn to praise God for creating us as we are, we will have difficulty discerning God's full longing for us.

Name some positive things about being a gay or lesbian Christian.

The author of Hebrews tells us to "continually offer a sacrifice of praise to God" (Heb. 13:15). Praising God for the things in our lives that feel good is easy. Praising God for those things that bring us trouble is much harder. We make a sacrifice of praise when we praise God for our sexual orientation because it is difficult to do. What do you sacrifice when you praise God for making you lesbian or gay? Write a short prayer thanking God for making you who you are.

MEDITATION

Memorize the prayer of gratitude you wrote earlier. Then spend a few moments quieting your mind and turning your attention to God. Say your prayer. You may find it difficult at first to be genuinely grateful. Ask God to give you gratitude.

DAY FOUR ❋ **Discerning God's Presence in Coming Out**

Because heterosexuality is the "default value" in our culture, coming out is a lifelong process. Whether coming out to someone close to us or someone distant from us, we bring to that moment the gift of honesty. We open the door for a more intimate relationship with the other person. We also risk rejection, assault, derogation, or indifference.

Coming out is scary. Think of the person with whom you are least eager to discuss your sexual orientation. What are your fears about this conversation?

God yearns to be with us in our most difficult and terrifying moments. The author of Hebrews writes: "So we can say with confidence, 'The Lord is my helper; I will not be afraid. What can anyone do to me?'" (Heb. 13:6). What can you do to be aware of God's loving, guiding presence in these conversations? How would coming out be different if you were aware of God's presence?

MEDITATION

Spend a few moments reviewing a past conversation that was particularly difficult. Ask God to help you know divine comfort and strength as you review that memory.

DAY FIVE ✳ ## Discerning God's Presence in Relationships and Sexual Activities

Much of what has been described as a divinely ordained primary relationship reflects cultural mores rather than God's will. These principles typically include marriage between opposite sex persons, sex only within marriage, and sex only for the procreation of children. We are denied the sacrament of marriage, yet are condemned for being promiscuous. We struggle to understand our relationships as holy social institutions, blessed by God.

Consequently, we have few guidelines about the "right" behavior. We wonder if our same-sex relationships have standing in the eyes of God. We wonder about the role of sex in our lives.

Yet, God longs to saturate our lives—all of our lives.

Spend a few moments sitting quietly, allowing your mind to stay open. Ask God to reveal God's longing for you in this area of your life. Picture yourself in the sort of relationship God yearns for you to have. What do you suppose God wants for you in your intimate relationship?

What sort of sex do you think God longs for you to have? What criteria might you use to decide how to conduct your sexual behavior?

MEDITATION

Ask God to be present and to make you aware of God's presence in your primary relationship.

DAY SIX ❈ **Letting Go of Our Preconceived Ideas**

As we surrender more parts of our life to God, our ability to respond to the Spirit's promptings increases. We become more pliable in God's hands. Our longing for God joins with God's longing for us and creates a sweet union that guides us and keeps us.

But because our lives are shaped by oppression, discrimination, and threats to our well-being, we protect ourselves by creating limits for ourselves. These limits then become preconceived ideas about what can and cannot happen in our lives. For example, we might think, "I won't go to that church because it is full of homophobic people," or "I would be harassed if I lived anywhere but this neighborhood," What preconceived ideas do you have about your life?

Yet in order to hear God's call, we must repent of our preconceived ideas. Only then will we be sufficiently pliable in God's hands. For lesbian and gay Christians, repentance of our self-imposed limits in response to the world's oppression is scary and full of risks. What would you risk if you were to repent of the preconceived ideas you identified above?

MEDITATION

"For God did not give us a spirit of cowardice, but rather a spirit of power and of love and of self-discipline" (2 Tim. 1:7). Ask God to give you a spirit of power and love and self-discipline, so that you might surrender your self-imposed limits to God.

DAY SEVEN ❧ **Evaluating Our Alternatives**

By embracing God's presence in every part of our lives and repenting of our preconceived ideas about the limits on our lives, we become less attached to things of the world and more attached to things of God. We are more receptive to God's way for us. We hear God's voice more clearly and know God's way more surely.

When we take God's ownership of our lives seriously and become more responsive to God's ways, God responds by leading us into a new life. God's way for us does not look like our parents' way for us, our culture's way for us, or our own ideas about our way. Consequently, as we explore God's new life for us we violate cultural, familial, and even our own expectations and boundaries. Our initial emotional response to God's invitation into a new way of living is anxiety.

Have you ever followed God's call to do something even though it made you anxious? What was that like for you? How long were you anxious? How did it turn out?

The prophet Isaiah tells us that God says: "Listen carefully to me, and eat what is good, and delight your-selves in rich food" (Isa. 22:2b). Although our initial response to listening carefully to God and eating what is good is anxiety, we will eventually delight ourselves in the rich food of God's will for us. This is how we know we are correctly responding to God: an ultimate sense of consolation, peace, and love. Write about a time in which you made a difficult decision that ultimately resulted in divine peace.

MEDITATION

Ask God to give you the wisdom to eat the rich food of God's will and to infuse your life with God's delight.

Week Seven

MEMBERS OF THE
BODY OF CHRIST

Early church experiences were rich with meaning for many of us. Our relationships within the church were as formative and significant as our early family relationships. Our memories are full of smells, sounds, images, and feelings. We remember the music and the potluck dinners. We also remember the Bible stories, choir practice, baptisms, and the clean feeling inside of us after a particularly compelling worship service. No matter how estranged we become from the church, our early emotional ties to the church continue to tug at us.

We also have theological reasons for continuing our participation in the church. We were baptized into the church, and we may believe that we cannot be disciples of Christ apart from the body of Christ. Not only do we have strong emotional and psychological bonds to the church, the full flowering of our discipleship requires our ongoing participation in a worshipping community with other believers.

Given these strong attractions, our condemnation and rejection by the church creates a predicament for us. Our predicament is that the community into which our love of God draws us is the primary source of the homophobia in our lives. The place we feel most at home on one level is the place we are most estranged at another level. Lesbian and gay Christians attempt to resolve this dilemma in many different ways.

Some of us abandon Christianity altogether. Others of us sustain our identities as Christians, but swear off church. We decide that if they won't accept us, we won't accept them. Some of us continue in our home churches, our sexual orientation hidden. Others attend a different mainline church, but never acknowledge our partner and family. Still others of us abandon the church of our youth for churches whose primary parishioners are lesbian and gay Christians, or those few mainline churches who welcome us. None of these options is without pain.

This week we will pray about and reflect on our relationship with the church, its rejection of us, and how we are called to respond.

Remember to start each day's reflection period with a short prayer for your prayer partner. You could pray the following:

I celebrate, loving Spirit, being in community with _____ . *I rejoice in our times together and pray that our gathering might always be in the name of your Son. Amen.*

DAY ONE ❋ Early Church Experiences

Worship and other church activities are built on rich imagery laden with emotion. We are exposed to a constant stream of pictures, stories, songs, and liturgies. Out of this mix, we develop a basic view of our world and ourselves.

Many times a particular Bible story shapes our basic view of the world. Alternatively, a Bible character or story might capture essential elements of early ways of seeing the world and ourselves. Do you recall a story or character that you found particularly compelling as a child? What did you like about the story or character? What was it about the story or character that impressed you?

Another source of influence in church is adults other than our parents. These people might include a pastor, a Sunday school teacher, the parent of a friend, or some other adult. Do you remember any influential adults from your church? What were they like? Was their impact on you good or bad or both? How did they shape your ideas about church, about God, about people?

MEDITATION

Resting quietly, close your eyes and let the images and memories of your early church experience run through your mind. Offer each of these memories and images to God, and ask God to give you wisdom and insight into the nature of these memories.

DAY TWO ❊ **Testing the Spirits**

Out of the stories we learn and the people we know as children in the church, we form certain beliefs, attitudes, values, and goals. We may also learn certain feelings in response to specific cues. A friend who sings in the choir experienced a profound peace as the organist improvised on "Jesus Loves Me" during a worship service. That particular song triggered feelings of comfort and safety in my friend. Other imagery may generate feelings that are destructive. For example, some churches use biblical imagery to elicit intense feelings of shame and guilt associated with sex.

As you remember early church experiences, identify the beliefs, attitudes, values, and goals your church experience created in you. Write these down. Then identify any intense feelings associated with these beliefs and values.

In 1 Corinthians 12:3, Paul informs the church at Corinth how to test a spirit: "Therefore I want you to understand that no one speaking by the Spirit of God ever says, 'Let Jesus be cursed' and no one can say 'Jesus is Lord' except by the Holy Spirit." In other words, the Spirit of God is always Christ-centered. Being Christ-centered means that the Spirit of God is characterized by love, self-sacrifice, service, healing, and generosity. Review the list you wrote above. What kind of spirit fuels the goals, values, and beliefs on that list? Do the various items on your list reflect a mixture of spirits? What are they?

MEDITATION

As you pray, ponder each of the items on your list. Thank God for those beliefs that reflect the Spirit of God. Ask God for deliverance from those values and ideas inspired by destructive spirits.

DAY THREE ❈ **Current Expectations of the Church**

In the twelfth chapter of 1 Corinthians, Paul describes the church as an organic whole, in which all members, gifts, services, activities, and ministries are equally valued. The church is the body of Christ: "Now you are the body of Christ and individually members of it" (1 Cor. 12:27). At the same time, the church is subject to the same sin, self-deception, hypocrisy, ignorance, and other shortcomings that mark all human social institutions.

The church is home to great evil as well as great good. We may wish that the church be a place of unconditional love and self-sacrifice. But when we expect only good from the church, we have unrealistic expectations. Do you have any unrealistic expectations concerning the church? If so, what are they?

Just as the body of Christ was broken on the cross, so too is today's body of Christ broken: over social justice issues, over abortion, over ordination of women or divorced men, and over our inclusion in the church. Because we are one of the major "issues" facing the church, our very existence contributes to the brokenness of the body of Christ. Consequently, we live this "issue" in a way heterosexual Christians will never know. We are identified with the source of the church's brokenness. How does this impact your experience of the church? Your expectations?

MEDITATION

Spend a few moments in silence and focus on your longing for God. Ask God to help you surrender your unrealistic expectations of the church and to give you the peace and courage to live with the church as it is.

DAY FOUR ❋ **One Body, Many Members**

One of the most divisive questions in the church today is whether "practicing homosexuals" can be a part of the church. Yet Paul suggests that our inclusion in the church cannot be questioned. In describing the church, he says "As it is, there are many members, yet one body. The eye cannot say to the hand, 'I have no need of you,' nor again the head to the feet, 'I have no need of you'" (1 Cor. 12:20–21).

This text suggests that one part of the church does not have the right to determine who is or is not part of the body of Christ. In God's eyes, we are all one body. Christ is the head of the church, and the church belongs to Christ and to Christ alone. Because we have been baptized into the body of Christ, we will always be part of the church.

Can you understand yourself as being chosen by Christ to be a part of the body of Christ? If not, what prevents you from seeing your relationship with the church in these terms? What helps you see the sovereignty of God and the lordship of Christ in church?

Reread verses 20 and 21. Draw a picture of your image of the church. Your image may be that of a body, or it may be some other image. Put a star on the part of the drawing that represents you.

MEDITATION

As you pray today, bring your picture of the body of Christ to God. Ask God to help you see the church through God's eyes.

DAY FIVE ❈ ## Who Needs Church, Anyway?

Sometimes we are so hurt and so fed up with peoples' cruelty and the abuse from church members, we want to leave and never come back. The thought of spending the rest of our lives in such a hostile environment is overwhelming. We wonder why we should stay in a community that so clearly rejects us. Have you ever left a church? Did you stay away? Come back later? Find a different church?

Read 1 Corinthians 12:14–20. In verse 15, Paul writes "If the foot would say, 'Because I am not a hand, I do not belong to the body,' that would not make it any less part of the body." This text suggests that we cannot disavow our membership in the church any more than another Christian can disavow us. Because we have been baptized into the body of Christ, we will always be part of the church. Even though we may feel like we are not part of them, in God's eyes we are all one body. How do you reconcile this text with the limited choices we have for church participation?

MEDITATION

Bring to God your pain over the church's rejection of you. Bring your problem of belonging to a body that disavows you. Bring your own desire to reject the church. Ask God for direction in your church involvement.

DAY SIX ❋ The Appearance of Weakness

Because "our role in the church" is such a frequent and divisive topic, we appear to be weaker members in the body of Christ—a source of acrimony and distraction from the church's larger mission. Many sisters and brothers wish we would just go away and quit being a source of trouble.

And yet, Paul gives us a different picture. He says "On the contrary, the members of the body that seem to be weaker are indispensable" (1 Cor. 12:22). If we are the members of the body of Christ who appear to be weaker, then we are not only included in the body of Christ, we are indispensable to the larger church. A major Pauline theme is how God's power, strength, and grace is made most manifest in weakness. Given this theme, how would you interpret our appearance of weakness?

Do lesbian and gay Christians have a special gift or indispensable calling to the church at this time? What might that gift be? How are we indispensable to the body of Christ?

MEDITATION

Ask God to show you how you are indispensable to your local church, what special grace you bring to the particular embodiment of the body of Christ in your life.

DAY SEVEN   ❈   **Spiritual Gifts**

In 1 Corinthians 12:4–11, Paul talks about the variety of gifts given by the Spirit. In verse 7 he writes, "To each is given the manifestation of the Spirit for the common good." God gives each person baptized into the church a spiritual gift for the upbuilding and good of the body of Christ. This text suggests we each have invaluable gifts for the edification of our church community.

We have been so shamed and abused by the church, we may have difficulty believing that we have been given spiritual gifts. Yet the distribution of gifts is dependent upon God, not on us or those who judge us. In verse 11, Paul writes, "All these are activated by one and the same Spirit, who allots to each one individually just as the Spirit chooses." The Spirit chooses how gifts are allotted. And the Spirit chooses to allot gifts to straight and gay Christians alike. Recall specific ways in which you served your church community. What is (are) your spiritual gift(s)? How have you used them for the good of the church?

Sometimes we cannot use our gift(s) because the church will not receive them. One example is the church that refuses to ordain women or lesbian or gay Christians. When we do not exercise our gifts for the good of the church, we deprive the church of a God-given gift. When the church rejects us, the church rejects a gift of the Spirit. Have you ever had the experience of not being allowed to use your spiritual gifts? Are you still responsible to God for using your gifts for the good of the church even if the church rejects you?

MEDITATION

As you pray today, thank God for the Spirit's gifts to you. Ask God how you might contribute your gifts to the church.

Week Eight — OUR WITNESS TO LIVING IN CHRIST

A s gay and lesbian Christians, we are called to embrace two realities: our God-given sexual orientation and our God-given life in Christ Jesus. Both are gifts from our Creator. For the most part, however, our environments are hostile to one of these two gifts from God. To many of our gay brothers and lesbian sisters, our Christian discipleship is at best inexplicable and at worst a betrayal of our fight for civil rights. To many of our Christian sisters and brothers, our sexual orientation is at worst a sin against God and at best a mystery. Life is usually easier when we keep either our sexual orientation or our Christian discipleship in the closet.

Just as the crucifixion of Jesus did not fit into anyone's ideas of God's activity in the world, neither do our lives fit into the world's ideas about Christian discipleship and authentic living. When we bear witness to our sexual orientation as well as living our life in Christ, we embody the manifestation of God's love in the shame of the cross. We become an expression of God's glory and presence in what the world considers shameful, of God's power in our weakness, of God's love and forgiveness in response to the world's hate.

An important component of our witness is coming out. Because we have no civil rights, and because we have no standing in the church, coming out as lesbian and gay persons is generally more risky than coming out as Christians. Every time we come out in a new situation or in a new relationship, we make ourselves vulnerable. We risk crucifixion. Over a lifetime of coming out, we risk jobs, status, relationships, maybe even our families. When we accept the life God has given us and claim that life publicly, we sacrifice the life we planned for ourselves. Instead, we turn towards the life God wants for us. In so doing, we become a living sacrifice. Our lives become an act of worship.

As with any sacrifice, coming out can be difficult and painful. This week we will consider our experiences with coming out, reflect on our fears about risking crucifixion, and explore how God's love, glory, power, and forgiveness are manifested when we come out to other people in our world.

Remember to start each day's reflection period with a short prayer for your prayer partner. You could pray the following:

Thank you, holy Father, Mother of us all, for the life of _____ . Give us the strength to remain the salt of the earth and a light in the darkness. Amen.

DAY ONE ❊ **Doing It God's Way**

"When the days drew near for him to be taken up, he set his face to go to Jerusalem" (Luke 9:51). Jesus was leaving Galilee to go to Jerusalem. Jesus left behind his popular ministry of healing, teaching, and feeding people and "set his face" to Jerusalem. Going to Jerusalem made Jesus vulnerable to unknown threats. By going to Jerusalem, Jesus risked crucifixion. But God wanted him in Jerusalem. So despite the danger, Jesus "set his face to go to Jerusalem." Jesus decided to live his life God's way. He put his future into God's hands.

When we are honest about our sexual orientation with those around us, we give up trying to live the life we think we should live. Instead, we become open to living our life God's way. We sacrifice our expectations about how we spend our lives, and commit ourselves to God's way for us.

Think of some relationship or area of your life in which you remain in the closet. If you were to come out in that relationship, what would you sacrifice? What dreams, social standing, relationships, or ambitions do you risk losing? Sometimes we are out in all areas of our lives. However, we avoid environments (like church or certain occupations) where being out is a problem. Is that true for you? What environment do you avoid?

If you were to commit to God's way in this relationship or area of your life, what would you do differently? How would your behavior and conversation change?

MEDITATION

Bring this most avoided or closeted area of your life before God in prayer. Ask God to help you sacrifice your ideas about your life to God and to help you to do it God's way.

DAY TWO ❀ Frightening Fantasies

The reality of the persecution of lesbian and gay persons feeds our fantasies about what would happen if we were to come out in a situation. But we not only imagine rejection or persecution based on the very real heterosexism expressed in our culture, we also project old fears and memories of rejection, abuse, and abandonment onto the act of coming out. Do you have early experiences of abuse, abandonment, or rejection? What memories come to mind? Do any of the accompanying feelings surface when you consider coming out in a current situation? What are they?

What are the similarities between the old situation of rejection and abuse and the current circumstances surrounding the area of your life in which you are closeted? Are the people similar? How are they different? How are the two situations different? Do you have more resources?

MEDITATION

Thinking about the part of your life lived in the closet, pray this prayer: "Save me, O Lord, from my enemies; I have fled to you for refuge. Teach me to do your will, for you are my God. Let your good spirit lead me on a level path" (Ps. 143:9, 10).

DAY THREE   ❋   **Risking Crucifixion**

Every time we come out to a new person, we risk crucifixion. Many of us have had very bad experiences as a result of coming out. Most of us know, firsthand, the negative consequences of being authentic as a lesbian or gay person in a hostile environment. We have lost jobs, apartments, and scholarships. Parents have disowned us, siblings have threatened us, and our offspring have prevented us from seeing our grandchildren. Sometimes ministers have castigated us and lifelong friends have shunned us. Too many times the courts have taken our children away.

What was your worst experience in coming out? How did you feel about the situation then? Now?

In 1 Peter we read: "But even if you do suffer for doing what is right, you are blessed. Do not fear what they fear, and do not be intimidated, but in your hearts sanctify Christ as Lord" (1 Pet. 3:14–15a). As you recall suffering for doing what is right, how were you blessed? What were "their" fears? Did you fear the same thing? Were you intimidated? Are you intimidated now?

MEDITATION

The author of I Peter tells us to sanctify Christ as Lord in our hearts. This means that Christ dominates our heart, our will, in our suffering. Bring your past sufferings to God and ask God to make Christ the Lord of your heart.

DAY FOUR ❋ Blessings

In the book of Esther, Esther marries King Ahasueras without disclosing her Jewish ancestry. She stays in the closet as a Jew. But when her people are threatened with extinction, Esther decides she must come out to her husband in order to save her people. She takes a great risk by coming out to her husband. Instead of punishing her for speaking out, King Ahasueras honors her and gives her people the protection she requests (see Esth. 8:1).

In the same way, some people honor our risk taking and vulnerability by blessing us when we come out to her or him. Recall some instance in which another person blessed you when you came out to them. What was that like? What were your feelings? Where you surprised by that person's response?

Sometimes being "out" as a lesbian or gay person gives us the opportunity to speak up for our people. Sometimes we are in the right place at the right time to ask for justice for lesbian and gay persons. Have you ever had that opportunity? Were you scared? How did you decide to respond to the opportunity? Were you successful in your quest for justice?

MEDITATION

Say a prayer of thanksgiving for those people in your life who have affirmed you as a lesbian or gay person. Thank God for those times of blessing and ask God to use them to embolden your witness.

DAY FIVE ❈ **A Living Sacrifice**

Living our life God's way by witnessing to our God-given sexual orientation as well as our God-given life in Christ creates a painful tension. One response to the tension is to absorb the shame and rejection others heap on us. An alternative response is to become bitter and angry, hardening our hearts toward our Christian sisters and brothers. In other words, we either draw the pain and shame inwards, or we throw it outwards.

Paul tells us that we are liberated from living in the flesh when we live in Christ. In the first two verses of Romans 12, Paul writes: "Present your bodies as a living sacrifice, holy and acceptable to God, which is your spiritual worship. Do not be conformed to this world, but be transformed by the renewing of your minds" (Rom. 12:1b–2a). Our willingness to witness to God's gifts and bear the resulting tension is a sacrifice we can make to God. Our lives become a living sacrifice, an act of worship and praise to our Creator and Redeemer. Have you ever had the experience of being a living sacrifice in and for a community?

Being conformed to this world is responding with shame toward ourselves or blame toward others. But when we live in Christ, we are transformed; we are liberated from these two very human responses. As we offer ourselves as a living sacrifice, over time God renews our minds into a transformed way of living. When Christ lives in us, we can offer our shame and our bitterness to God as a continual sacrifice. Our offering transforms us in a life lived deeper and deeper in Christ. What do you think it would be like to be completely transformed by the renewing of your mind? How would the act of coming out be different for you?

MEDITATION

Mentally review coming out events in your life and your feelings associated with them. Ask God to show you how to offer your body as a living sacrifice in your current relationships. Ask that your mind be transformed.

DAY SIX ❋ God's Strength in Our Weakness

In Judges 6:33–34, God had chosen Gideon to rout the Midianites from the Israelites' land. But God wanted the Israelites to give God the credit for the victory. Consequently, God didn't want Gideon to have so many troops. "The Lord said to Gideon, 'The troops with you are too many for me to give the Midianites into their hand. Israel would only take the credit away from me, saying, "my own hand has delivered me"'" (Judg. 7:2). So God instructed Gideon to keep only three hundred warriors for the battle. When Gideon and his diminished troops successfully routed the Midianites, God's hand in history was obvious and God received the glory.

Many times we are afraid to come out in a relationship or context because we are afraid to give up power. We are afraid we will lose a job, have our children taken away from us, or be kicked out of our church. We are afraid we will lose power in our lives and over our lives. Do you have any relationships or contexts in your current life in which you are afraid of losing power if you come out? What are they? What are you afraid will happen?

Sometimes God calls us to witness to our God-given gift of sexual orientation despite the resulting loss of power and privilege. How would you know if God were calling you into this kind of witness in one of the situations you identified earlier? How would God's power be made manifest?

MEDITATION

In today's prayer, ask God to show you how God's power can be made manifest in some specific area of your life.

DAY SEVEN ❈ **Boasting in the Lord**

In addition to power and privilege, we risk our honor when we come out as lesbian and gay Christians. We risk the respect and esteem others pay us. To many people, none of our other achievements or attributes matter if they know we are lesbian or gay persons. We cease being a person and become an issue.

Being labeled is dehumanizing and demeaning. Sometimes we are flooded with shame, and our self-esteem collapses. Because these effects are so painful, we avoid coming out where we think others will so label us. Have you ever had the experience of becoming an issue instead of a person? What was that like for you? Do you avoid coming out in certain situations and to certain people because you are afraid of becoming an issue?

"'Let the one who boasts, boast in the Lord.' For it is not those who commend themselves that are approved, but those whom the Lord commends" (2 Cor. 10:17–18).

Despite the risk of being dehumanized and humiliated, God sometimes calls on us to come out in a particular situation that harbors painful consequences. In an act of radical obedience, we embody not commending ourselves. Instead of defending (boasting in) ourselves, we boast in the Lord.

In order to make this happen, we have to give up defending ourselves. We trust God to be with us and nurture us in whatever unfolds. Although our sacrifice is great, our witness is powerful and the subsequent communion with God is intense. Think of a particularly difficult situation. Can you imagine not defending yourself? What would you have to sacrifice?

MEDITATION

Bring to God all those things you would have to sacrifice in order to boast only in the Lord. Ask God to lead you and teach you in this form of radical discipleship.

WITNESS INSPIRED BY THE HOLY SPIRIT

As lesbian and gay Christians, we face a lifetime of discrimination and conflict. For those of us who do not confront barriers based on our looks (i.e., those of us who are white or male), the intensity of persecution and discrimination we face is a shock. Because we are not accustomed to being the recipients of systemic discrimination, our first struggle is to come to terms with the inevitability of oppression in our lives.

Others of us have already experienced discrimination for our gender or our race. Although we have some experience in dealing with systemic racism or sexism, the added burden of living as a gay or lesbian person can be overwhelming. Not surprisingly, large numbers of our community live with depression and heightened levels of anxiety. As resilient or courageous as we might be, the overwhelming oppression we face each day in most areas of our lives makes us particularly prone to despair. As lesbian and gay Christians, however, we have a source of courage beyond ourselves.

The first disciples also needed courage after Jesus left them. They gathered in an upper room in Jerusalem and prayed. Eventually a loud sound like a violent wind filled the house. "All of them were filled with the Holy Spirit and began to speak in other languages, as the Spirit gave them ability" (Acts 2:4). As Christians, we are filled with the same Holy Spirit today.

Filled with the Holy Spirit, we are given both the courage and the wisdom to witness to God's saving presence in the world. Although our hearts may quail when we consider the vicissitudes of living fully as a lesbian or gay Christian, our hope is sustained by God's promise of ultimate redemption. Along the way, we will encounter periods of grief, anxiety, and depression. But we can also find courage in God's living presence. We are filled with the Holy Spirit.

This week we will explore how we might become bold in our witness. We will seek to deepen our responsiveness to the Spirit. And we will consider how we might depend on the Holy Spirit's sustaining presence during our most difficult moments.

Remember to start each day's reflection period with a short prayer for your prayer partner. You could pray the following:

Holy One, bless the life of _____ . Make your Holy Spirit fall upon us. Let us both know your care. Give us your courage and strength to be an ongoing witness to your love and power. Amen.

DAY ONE ❋ Praying for Boldness

In the fourth chapter of Acts, Peter and John are called before the council to give an account of their witness. The council warned Peter and John to stop witnessing, on pain of punishment. When Peter and John were released and joined their sisters and brothers, the group prayed for boldness: "And now, Lord, look at their threats, and grant to your servants to speak your word with all boldness" (Acts 2:29).

When faced with a threat for proclaiming our discipleship as lesbian and gay Christians, our natural response is to ask God for protection or liberation from the threat. Has there been a time in your life when you asked God for protection? How did God answer your prayer?

These first disciples suggest an alternative to praying for protection, that is, to pray for boldness. We have an important resource when the persecution intensifies and those around us make larger efforts to silence us. We can ask that we speak God's word with all boldness. Reflecting on a particularly difficult situation, how do you think your approach to the situation would change if you were to pray for boldness?

MEDITATION

"When they had prayed, the place in which they were gathered together was shaken; and they were all filled with the Holy Spirit and spoke the word of God with boldness" (Acts 4:31). Imagine yourself in this group of early Christians. Pray to be filled with the Holy Spirit and to speak the word of God with boldness.

DAY TWO　✳　**Inspired Witness**

We are attacked from many angles. People accuse us of being unnatural, of being willful sinners, of being emotionally immature or psychologically sick. We spend a lot of time and energy constructing counter arguments. We spend many hours in scientific research, biblical research, and psychological research. Government leaders, church leaders, and other social institutions repeatedly introduce legislation that deprives us of civil rights and ecclesial standing. In order to protect ourselves, we spend much of our time and energy rebutting those who attack us.

While these efforts are essential, lesbian and gay Christians are also called into a different way of responding. Talking to his disciples about how they are to behave during persecution, Jesus says, "So make up your minds not to prepare your defense in advance; for I will give you words and a wisdom that none of your opponents will be able to withstand or contradict" (Luke 21:14–15). When you apply his admonition to your own situation, what do you think he means? Is he saying not to do the research? Is he saying not to depend on the research? How does this change your approach?

When we are constantly defending ourselves against the charges of our enemies, we spend all of our time and energy on their arguments. We are shaped by their agenda for us, not by God's agenda for us. How do you see your own identity being shaped by the agenda of your enemies? In your family? In your job? In your church?

MEDITATION

Ask God to give you the courage to "make up your mind in advance" to rely on God's words and wisdom for your defense.

DAY THREE ❈ Accepting Our Marginal Status

When we resist our marginal status, resentment and fear and wishing it weren't so can consume us. The focus of our lives can be a bitterness that hardens our hearts and creates a continual hostility toward others. Do you resist your marginal status? Are you resentful? In denial? How do you feel sorry for yourself?

Ironically, in order to be bold in our witness, we must accept the fact that we are a marginal people with no rights. Paul, the bold apostle to the Gentiles, understood this relationship between resignation and boldness. After describing a vision of heaven, he tells of a thorn in his flesh: "Three times I appealed to the Lord about this, that it would leave me" (2 Cor. 12:8). Paul is begging God to remove something from his life that is a constant irritant, a continual source of pain, difficulty, and shame. Have you ever asked God to remove your thorn in the flesh? Your marginal status? How did you approach God? Are you still asking God to remove the thorn in your flesh?

MEDITATION

When the angel came to Mary and told her that she would bear a son, Mary's response was: "Here I am, the servant of the Lord; let it be with me according to your word" (Luke 1:38). As you pray today, repeat these words of Mary.

DAY FOUR ❋ **The Benefits of Powerlessness**

When Paul asked God to remove the thorn in his flesh, God said to him: "My grace is sufficient for you, for power is made perfect in weakness" (2 Cor. 12:9a). One benefit of being marginal people is that we have the opportunity to see God's power more frequently. If we had as much power as people in the center of our culture, our own power would take up our world and crowd out any possibility of knowing God's power.

When was the last time God's grace was sufficient for you in a situation? How was God's power made perfect in that time of weakness?

Paul continues: "So, I will boast all the more gladly of my weaknesses, so that the power of Christ may dwell in me. Therefore I am content with weaknesses, insults, hardships, persecutions, and calamities for the sake of Christ; for whenever I am weak, then I am strong" (2 Cor. 12:9b–10). Think of a situation in which your position is particularly precarious, in which you are in a weak position. In the space below, boast of your weakness in that situation. How does the power of Christ dwell in you?

MEDITATION

Ask God to show you God's power in those helpless areas of your life.

DAY FIVE ❀ ## The Sharing of His Suffering

Because we are the target of so much abuse, we typically suffer more than our straight sisters and brothers. The invisibility of our abuse adds to the intensity of our pain. And yet, we are called to proclaim the good news, even though our public witness makes us vulnerable to more abuse, and more suffering.

In another irony, we are less likely to be bold in our witness the more we resist suffering. This does not mean we are to seek out occasions to suffer. Nor do we deny the pain of our suffering. But we don't dwell on the unfairness of our suffering, nor do we try to hold our suffering at bay by denial. However, both responses are typical human ways to respond to suffering. Have there been times when you have been wrapped up in the unfairness of your suffering? Times when you denied that you were suffering?

Instead of resisting suffering, we embrace our suffering as an opportunity to participate in the sufferings of Christ. Paul says: "I want to know Christ and the power of his resurrection and the sharing of his suffering by becoming like him in his death" (Phil. 3:10). How might you know Christ in your suffering? Have you ever been drawn closer to Christ as a result of suffering?

MEDITATION

Identify an area of witness that you have not yet entered due to the potential suffering involved. With a crucifix, or a picture of a crucifix, bring this area to the foot of the cross. Ask God to join you with Christ in your sufferings.

DAY SIX ❁ The Benefits of Suffering

Not only will God teach us to accept suffering, we can also learn the benefits of suffering and thank God for those benefits. In his opening lines to the Corinthians, Paul says: "Blessed be the God and Father of our Lord Jesus Christ, the Father of mercies and the God of all consolations, who consoles us in all our affliction, so that we may be able to console those who are in any affliction with the consolation with which we ourselves are consoled by God" (2 Cor. 1:3–4).

Just as we receive consolation in our suffering, our suffering helps us console others. We become more empathetic with others, particularly people who are different from us. Suffering and knowing God's consolation create compassion in us for others' pain. We can offer them God's consolation. Think of a time when your empathy and compassion for another was a result of God's consolation of you. What was the relationship between your own suffering and your compassion for the suffering of the other person?

Paul continues: "For just as the sufferings of Christ are abundant for us, so also our consolation is abundant through Christ" (2 Cor. 1:5). When our witness creates an abundant suffering with Christ, this text promises us that we will receive abundant consolation. The secret of abundant consolation in suffering is suffering in and with Christ. What do you think it means to suffer with Christ?

MEDITATION

Bring a particular pain or suffering to God and ask God to use that suffering to give you compassion for others.

DAY SEVEN ❋ **Loving Our Enemies**

"Love your enemies, do good to those who hate you, bless those who curse you, pray for those who abuse you. If anyone strikes you on the cheek, offer the other also" (Luke 6:27–29a).

Some people protest that this text promotes passivity in the face of discrimination and persecution. These verses have been cited to persuade women to passively accept domestic violence in their homes, to convince African Americans to accept second-class citizenship in this country, and to dissuade lesbian and gay Christians from disturbing the church by witnessing to God's activity in our lives.

What do you think? Do you think that Jesus' command to love our enemies results in colluding with our own oppression? How have you seen this argument used in your own life?

When we examine this verse closely, we find Jesus telling us to engage in an active response to our enemies. Jesus tells us to do good to them, to bless them, to pray for them, and to turn our check. We don't run away. We don't curse them or fight back. Instead we insist on staying in the relationship and manifesting God's love in that relationship by loving them despite their hostile behavior. In God's power and love, we do not let them define themselves as enemies. Over time, such self-sacrifice manifests God's love in a particularly powerful way. Although loving our enemies is the core of our Christian vocation, it is full of challenges. Which of those challenges are particularly difficult for you?

MEDITATION

In today's prayer, bring your difficulties with loving your enemies and ask for forgiveness. Ask God to empower you to do those things that exemplify loving your enemies. Ask God to teach you to manifest God's love in self-sacrifice.

BENEDICTION AND DISPERSAL

We have come a long way during these past weeks. We began our journey by looking into the past to reflect on our story of faith. We probed and searched our hearts to discover the object of our devotion. We reviewed the people and events that shaped our lives, and we examined the longings of our hearts. In the second week, we re-visited our images of God. We poured over scripture, praying that God would re-place distorted images of God with realistic, Bible-based images of God. The pres-ence and healing power of Jesus Christ was the center of our attention during the third week. We sorted out the differences between those things that are sins in our lives and those things that others claim to be our sins. We once again experienced the healing power of forgiveness and renewed our identity in Christ Jesus.

In the fourth week we explored our relationship with the Bible. We considered the nature of inspiration and examined different ways of reading the Bible. We used our new skills to revisit a couple of "clobber" passages—texts traditionally used to exclude us. We pondered the ironies of how those clobber passages are used against us. In the fifth and sixth weeks we explored how the "false self" interferes with two related spiritual disciplines: prayer and discernment. In distinguishing between God's claim on our lives and who we think we should be, we were drawn closer to God and God's will for us. We learned to ignore fears and assumptions born of homophobia in order to hear God's will for us.

During the seventh week, we studied Paul's understanding of the church. We found that our own presence within the church, as the ones who appear to be weak, is indispensable to the church. We asked God to guide our participation in the church. The eighth week was devoted to our lifelong witness to our sexual orientation and God's presence in our lives. We explored our fears of coming out. We recalled good memories associated with coming out. We investigated how our powerlessness and shame can be a witness to God's power and glory. We learned to boast in the Lord and find our confidence in God. In the last week, we asked the Holy Spirit to so fill our lives that we might be bold in our witness to God's love and generosity. We learned that in our suffering we can suffer with Christ. Finally, we contemplated how we might love our enemies.

As lesbian and gay Christians, we have a unique opportunity to be Christ-like: to love those who act as our enemies. With each hostile encounter, with each difficult situation, we are cocrucified with Christ. In Christ, we can love those who dehumanize us. But our love doesn't come from ourselves. We can only love with Christ's love. Our love is not a personal virtue. Rather, our love is born of Christ's love in us and for us. In Christ, we can love in ways we could never love without Christ.

As a living sacrifice, we become increasingly conformed to the mind of Christ. Over time, we are transformed. Our lives are more and more consumed by the self-giving love of Jesus Christ. As our lives deepen in Christ, we become icons, portals to God's love in the world. Our witness to the faith of Jesus Christ and the righteousness of God draws others into the arms of our Creator. Our witness speaks to people who might otherwise never know the saving grace of our Redeemer.

We have a particular witness to make in the world: a witness to the no-holds-barred love of God in Jesus Christ. Like Jesus, our witness is to those in the religious establishment who want to crucify us. Also like Jesus, our witness is to those who do not yet know the sweet communion of God's love in Christ. Our lives can create an opportunity for people from both of these groups to know God's grace and healing power.

I hope you have made some discoveries about your spirituality and developed insight into your faith journey as a result of these last nine weeks of study and prayer. I also know that working through this workbook does not answer all your questions or resolve all your challenges. My prayer is that your work with these exercises has launched you into a renewed sense of discipleship. God is working in you and through you. As you continue to grow in Christian discipleship, God will illuminate your lingering questions. You belong to God in Christ Jesus, and you are God's beloved. You are created to be a witness to the one Creator, the one source of all love.

To this end we always pray for you, asking that our God will make you worthy of his call and will fulfill by his power every good resolve and work of faith, so that the name of our Lord Jesus may be glorified in you, and you in him, according to the grace of our God and the Lord Jesus Christ (2 Thess. 1:11–12).

RESOURCES (Annotated)

HOMOSEXUALITY AND THE CHURCH

John J. McNeill, *The Church and the Homosexual,* 4th ed. (Boston: Beacon Press, 1993).

In this classic work, Father McNeill addresses homophobic arguments embedded within moral theology, scripture, church tradition, and human sciences. He exposes their flaws and suggests less biased understandings. Although this book is helpful for all Christians, his arguments are particularly compelling for persons with a Roman Catholic background.

Letha Scanzoni and Virginia Mollenkott, *Is the Homosexual My Neighbor? A Positive Christian Response* (San Francisco: HarperSanFrancisco, 1994).

The authors examine biblical and psychological understanding of homosexuality, as well as the tendency to stigmatize and stereotype others. They challenge us as Christians to rethink our views on homosexuality and suggest a morality and spirituality for lesbian and gay Christians.

Online The Other Side—Christian GLBT resource page
www.theotherside.org/resources/gay/links.html

This website gives links to all the organizations associated with the various denominations, links of ecumenical organizations, as well as a few primary secular organizations.

Religioustolerance.org
www.religioustolerance.org/hom_chur2.htm

This excellent site examines multiple issues related to religious tolerance. This particular section provides in-depth information on the stance of forty-four Christian denominations toward membership, ordination, and other involvement of lesbian and gay Christians. A particularly helpful resource.

The Center for Lesbian and Gay Studies in Religion and Ministry at Pacific School of Religion
http://www.clgs.org

A new organization whose mission is "to advance the well-being of lesbian, gay, bisexual, and transgendered people and to transform faith communities and the wider society by taking a leading role in shaping a new public discourse on religion and sexuality through education, research, community building, and advocacy," they are constructing a large website with many resources.

TWO STORIES

Mel White, *Stranger at the Gate: To Be Gay and Christian in America* (New York: Simon & Schuster, 1994).

White recounts his struggles growing up as a gay man passionate about his faith within a conservative, evangelical church. He documents the trials associated with trying to change himself into the person others told him he should be.

Mel White's website
www.melwhite.org
This site includes a copy of Walter Wink's *What the Bible Really Says About Homosexuality* that you can download.

Soul Force
www.soulforce.org
This organization was founded by Mel White to combat injustice against GLBTs in the church using nonviolent resistance.

Leroy Aarons, *Prayers for Bobby: A Mother's Coming to Terms with the Suicide of Her Gay Son* (San Francisco: HarperSanFrancisco, 1996).

After her son's suicide, Mary Griffith struggled with her pain and loss by examining the religious beliefs that contributed to her rejection of him as a gay man. This book is a painful and personal chronicle of her journey into acceptance and healing. She shares her most painful and intimate moments, hoping that other gay and lesbian persons do not have to die to get their parents' acceptance.

RESOURCES FOR DEEPENING CHRISTIAN SPIRITUALITY

Chris Glaser, *Come Home: Reclaiming Spirituality and Community As Gay Men and Lesbians,* 2nd ed. (Gaithersburg, Md.: Chi Rho Press, 1998).

Glaser invites lesbian, gay, bisexual, and transgendered Christians to become reconciled with our Christian roots and to return to our faith. In this book, he helps us to know that we are the beloved of God.

Chris Glaser, *The Word Is Out: Daily Reflections on the Bible for Lesbians and Gay Men* (Louisville: Westminster John Knox Press, 1999).

Daily, Bible-based meditations for lesbian and gay Christians.

William George Storey, ed., *A Book of Prayer: For Gay and Lesbian Christians* (New York: Crossroad/Herder & Herder, 2002).

In this book, Storey creates traditional morning and evening office prayers that reflect the themes of lesbian and gay life: coming-out, abandonment, holy union, and praying for our enemies. A good resource for Christians from a liturgical church tradition.

The Other Side: Strength for the Journey
300 West Apsley, Philadelphia, PA 19144; 800-700-9280 Fax: 215-849-3755

A bimonthly, ecumenical magazine established in 1965 to encourage those in the church's struggles to integrate. The group describe themselves as "advancing a healing Christian vision—a vision grounded in the redeeming ways of God." Their community is committed to encouraging and embodying the radically inclusive gospel.

Whosoever
www.whosoever.org

An online magazine for gay, lesbian, bisexual, and transgendered Christians. This monthly magazine has main articles, devotions, gay apologetics, lists of resources, and several forums.

Rainbow Christian Youth Ministry
www.rcym.org

This site is for GLBT young people who have been rejected by churches due to their sexuality. The founder is Steve Payne, youth pastor, who hopes to help young people learn that they can be young, gay, and Christian.

Christian Lesbians.com
www.christianlesbians.com

This site was created by a lesbian Christian with evangelical roots. The purpose of christianlesbians.com is three-fold: To proclaim the good news of Jesus' and God's unconditional and abiding love for all people; to offer information and resources for women who are struggling to reconcile their faith and sexuality and to let them know that God need not be forsaken simply because of their sexual orientation (God has definitely not forsaken you!); and to create a circle of fellowship and support for Christian lesbians, many of whom feel isolated by living in "the closet" or by the rejection of their family, friends, and their own church community.

COMING OUT

Mary V. Borhek, *Coming Out to Parents: A Two-Way Survival Guide for Lesbians and Gay Men and Their Parents* rev. ed. (Cleveland: Pilgrim Press, 1993).

A classic in the field since 1983, this book has helped countless lesbian and gay persons and their parents negotiate the sometimes painful, always difficult process of a family adjusting to a gay member. Worth studying.

Michelangelo Signorile, *Outing Yourself: How to Come Out as Lesbian or Gay to Your Family, Friends, and Coworkers* (New York: Fireside, 1996).

This book offers comprehensive guidance and structure for those in the process of coming out. Outing Yourself is helpful for those just beginning the journey as well as those who are further down the road. Signorile includes a fourteen-step program with exercises, meditation notes, and anger checks.

Donald H. Clark, *Loving Someone Gay,* 20th anniversary ed. (Berkeley, Calif.: Celestial Arts, 1997).

This classic is a good book to give family or friends after you have come out to them.

Parents, Families and Friends of Lesbians and Gays
www.pflag.org

PFLAG is a grassroots organization committed to providing support to the parents, families, and friends of lesbian and gay persons. Although this organization advocates for equality and justice, this is probably the best resource for parents looking for help and emotional support as they adjust to their offspring's sexual orientation.

You can download a PDF file of *Just the Facts: A Primer for Principals, Educators and School Personnel.*

Human Rights Campaign Resource Guide to Coming Out
www.hrc.org/ncop/guide/index.asp

The Human Rights Campaign is a national lobby and watchdog group for equality for GLBT citizens. This particular page of their web site has excellent resources to help you come out.

American Psychological Association Policy Statements on Lesbian and Gay Issues
www.apa.org/pi/statemen.html

Quoting obsolete materials and discredited behavioral scientists, some church organizations state that mental health professionals are of divided opinion about the mental health of lesbian and gay persons. This is misleading and untrue. Both the American Psychiatric Association and the American Psychological Association state clearly that homosexuality is *not* a mental illness. This web page gives you the American Psychological Association's official policy.

Answers to Your Questions About Sexual Orientation and Homosexuality—APA
www.apa.org/pubinfo/answers.html

This web page gives APA endorsed responses to commonly asked questions about sexual orientation and homosexuality. These answers reflect current findings of creditable behavioral scientists.

BIBLICAL INTERPRETATION RESOURCES

These references are only a few of the many books concerning interpretation of those scriptures typically used to exclude lesbian and gay Christians. You will find many more excellent references in your library or bookstore.

Daniel A. Helminiak, *What the Bible Really Says About Homosexuality* (San Francisco: Alamo Square Press, 2000).

Using current biblical research, Helminiak revisits the primary "clobber passages" and argues that the current condemnation of homosexuality results from faulty interpretative methods.

Robin Scroggs, *The New Testament and Homosexuality* (Philadelphia: Fortress Press, 1984).

Scroggs explores the meaning of homosexuality and pederastry within the Greco Roman world. He then examines scripture in light of his understanding of the culture that surrounded the early church. This book was one of the early, important works in the field of homosexuality and biblical interpretation.

David Balch, ed., *Homosexuality, Science, and the "Plain Sense" of Scripture* (Grand Rapids: William. B. Eerdmans Publishing, 2000).

This collection of papers is a good example of the give and take of biblical scholarship in considering the biblical witness. The papers in this book present multiple viewpoints and expose the reader to solid biblical research. These papers illustrate the how different scholars reach different conclusions from the same research. This book can be technical and is best read after reading several introductory texts.

RELATED TITLES AVAILABLE FROM THE PILGRIM PRESS

COMING OUT TO PARENTS

A Two-Way Survival Guide for Lesbians and Gay Men and Their Parents

MARY V. BORHEK

ISBN 0-8298-0957-0 / 310 pages / paper / $16.00

For lesbians and gays, this book explores the fears and misgivings accompanying their revelation to their parents and offers suggestions on how and when to come out, what reactions to expect, and how to deal with ensuing awkwardness. It guides parents through natural feelings of grief and loss and shows how understanding, compassion, and insight can lead to deeper love and acceptance.

COMING OUT THROUGH FIRE

Surviving the Trauma of Homophobia

LEANNE McCALL TIGERT AND TIMOTHY BROWN, EDS.

ISBN 0-8298-1293-8 / 148 pages / paper / $13.00

A book for lesbians, gays, bisexuals, and transgendered persons seeking to move through the trauma of homophobia with the passion and power of transformation. Also useful for pastors, therapists, and other counseling professionals who seek to confront prejudice and fear and further the process of healing and recovery in the church and the wider community.

COMING OUT WHILE STAYING IN
Struggles and Celebrations of Lesbians, Gays, and Bisexuals in the Church

LEANNE MCCALL TIGERT

ISBN 0-8298-1150-8 / 182 pages / paper / $15.00

Tigert reflects upon her own personal struggle with the church as a source of pain, alienation, support, and spiritual renewal, and shares others' struggles with the church in the hope of opening the doors to change, healing, and liberation for LGBT individuals.

COMING OUT YOUNG AND FAITHFUL

LEANNE MCCALL TIGERT AND TIMOTHY BROWN, EDS.

ISBN 0-8298-1414-0 / 112 pages / paper / $13.00

This groundbreaking collection comes from lesbian, gay, bisexual, transgender, and questioning teens who share their experiences in their communities and churches. Includes resources for ministry and advocacy to help open the doors of affirmation, love, and commitment to the needs of LGBT youth and young adults.

COURAGE TO LOVE
Liturgies for the Lesbian, Gay, Bisexual, and Transgender Community

GEOFFREY DUNCAN, ED.

ISBN 0-8298-1468-X / 384 pages / paper / $23.00

Winner of a 2002 Lambda Literary Award for Religion/Spirituality. An exceptional collection of worship and other liturgical resources inclusive of and sensitive to the LGBT community for both clergy and lay people. Beneficial for relationships with families, church, and community. Includes liturgies for the Eucharist and same-sex marriages.

THE ESSENTIAL GAY MYSTICS

ANDREW HARVEY, ED.

ISBN 0-8298-1443-4 / 304 pages / paper / $18.00

From Sappho to Whitman, Vergil to Audre Lorde, *The Essential Gay Mystics* is a collection of mystical writings covering the period from early Greek writers to the twentieth century. Contains over sixty selections celebrating those who love others of the same sex.

GAY THEOLOGY WITHOUT APOLOGY

GARY DAVID COMSTOCK

ISBN 0-8298-0944-9 / 184 pages / paper / $16.00

A case for the acknowledgement of varied expressions of humanity. Comstock presents essays that express a specific gay theology, which is an understanding of his personal concern for all people to recognize that there is a true benefit to fully appreciating gayness as a part of being both human and Christian.

To order these or any other books from The Pilgrim Press, call or write to:

THE PILGRIM PRESS
700 PROSPECT AVENUE
CLEVELAND, OH 44115-1100

Phone orders 800-537-3394 (M–F, 8:30AM–4:30PM ET)
Fax orders 216-736-2206
Please include shipping charges of $4.00 for the first book and 75¢ for each additional book.
Or order from our Web site at www.pilgrimpress.com.
Prices subject to change without notice.